BEST OF METALLICA FOR UKULELE

GW00645384

Arranged by Steve Gorenberg

Cherry Lane Music Company
Director of Publications/Project Editor: Mark Phillips

ISBN 978-1-60378-961-5

Visit our website at www.cherrylaneprint.com

BATTERY

Words and Music by
James Hetfield and Lars Ulrich

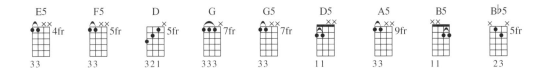

Intro
Moderately slow ♩ = 75

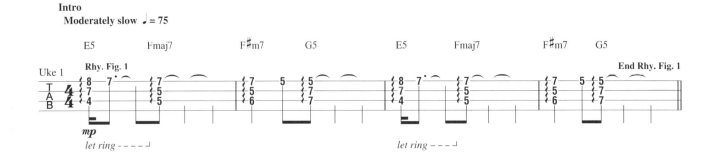

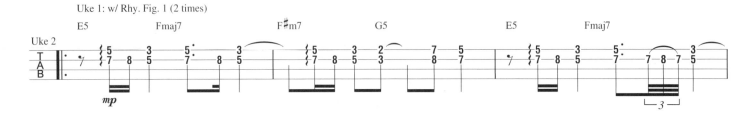

*See top of page for chord diagrams pertaining to rhythm slashes.

Fast Rock ♩ = 190

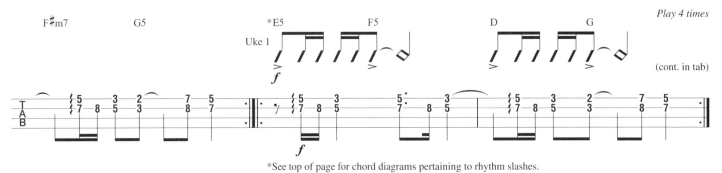

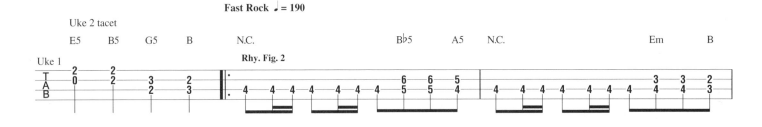

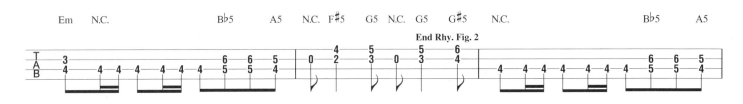

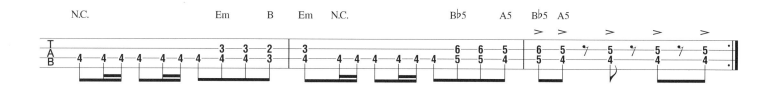

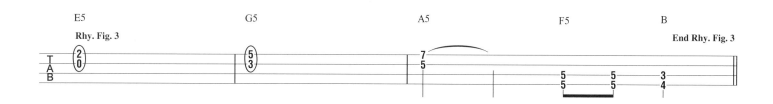

Verse

Uke 1: w/ Rhy. Fig. 2 (2 times)

1. Lash - ing out the ac - tion, re - turn - ing the re - ac - tion, weak are ripped and torn a -
2. Crush - ing all de - ceiv - ers, mash - ing non - be - liev - ers, nev - er - end - ing po - ten -
3. Cir - cle of de - struc - tion, ham - mer comes crush - ing, pow - er - house of en - er -

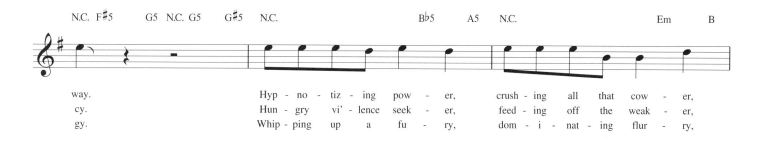

way.
cy.
gy.

Hyp - no - tiz - ing pow - er, crush - ing all that cow - er,
Hun - gry vi' - lence seek - er, feed - ing off the weak - er,
Whip - ping up a fu - ry, dom - i - nat - ing flur - ry,

Chorus

Uke 1: w/ Rhy. Fig. 3

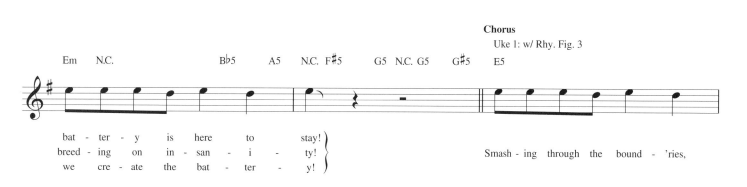

bat - ter - y is here to stay!
breed - ing on in - san - i - ty!
we cre - ate the bat - ter - y!

Smash - ing through the bound - 'ries,

Uke 1: w/ Rhy. Fig. 2

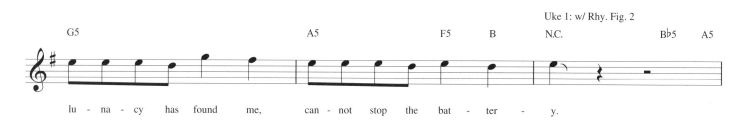

lu - na - cy has found me, can - not stop the bat - ter - y.

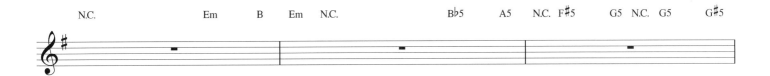

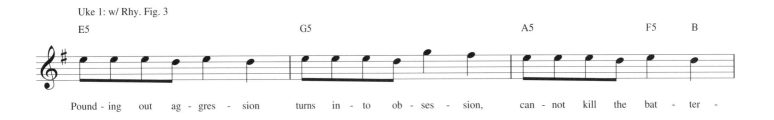

Uke 1: w/ Rhy. Fig. 3

Pound - ing out ag - gres - sion turns in - to ob - ses - sion, can - not kill the bat - ter -

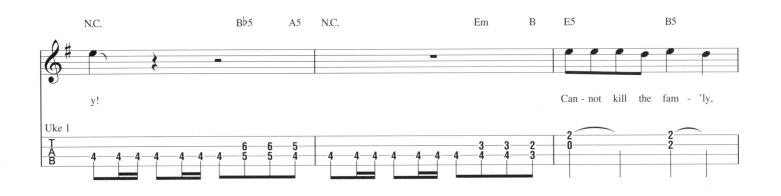

y!

Can - not kill the fam - 'ly,

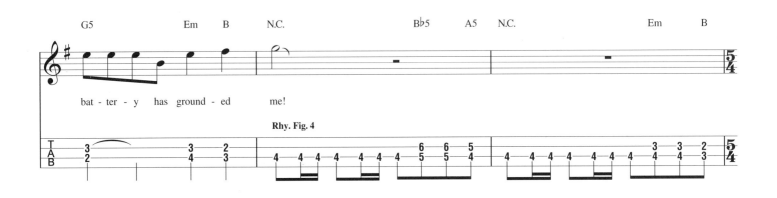

bat - ter - y has ground - ed me!

Rhy. Fig. 4

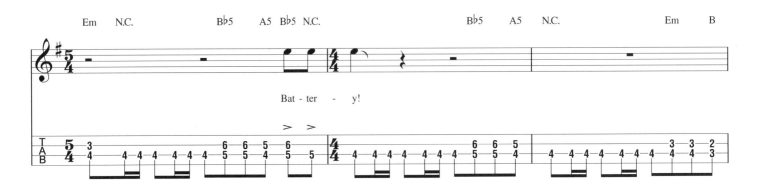

Bat - ter - y!

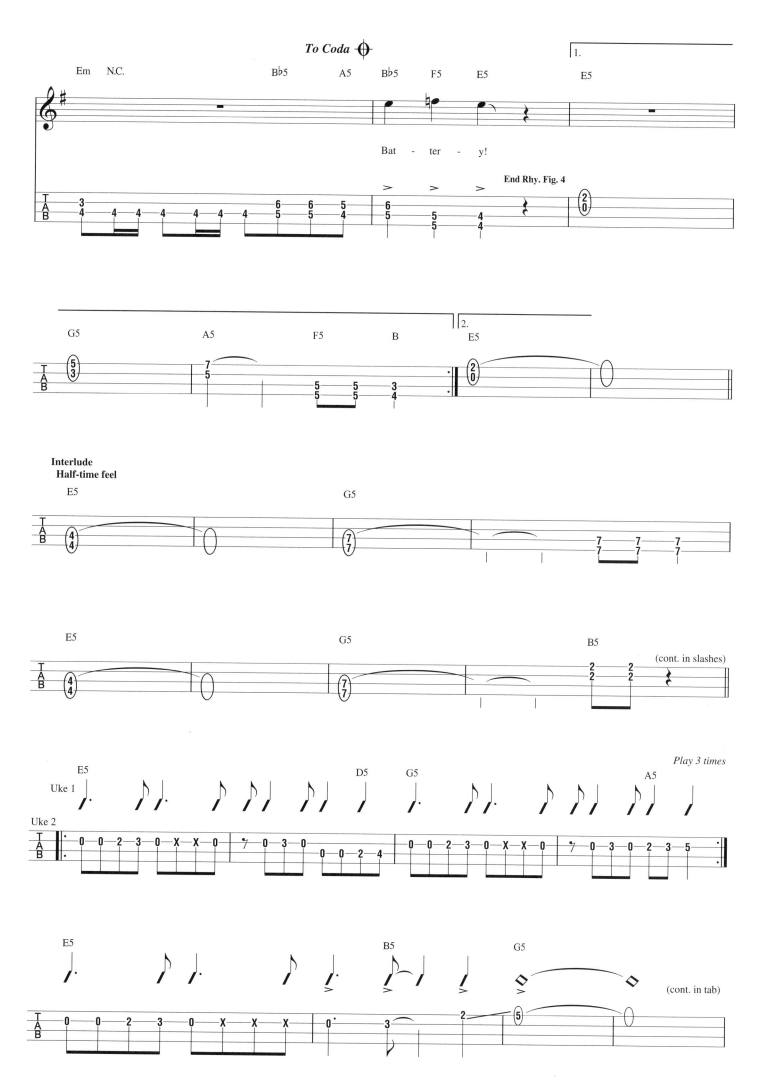

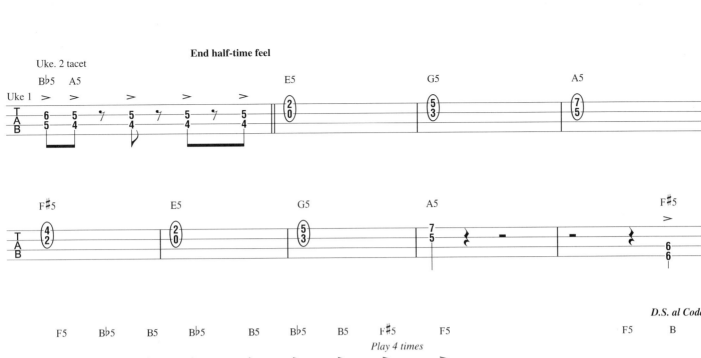

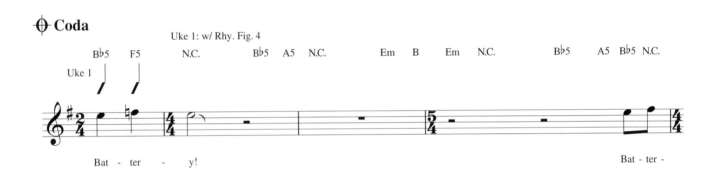

D.S. al Coda

Coda

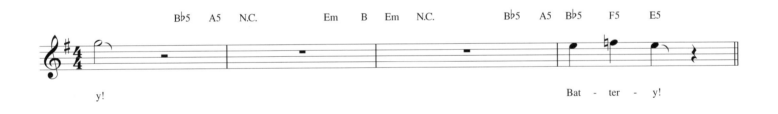

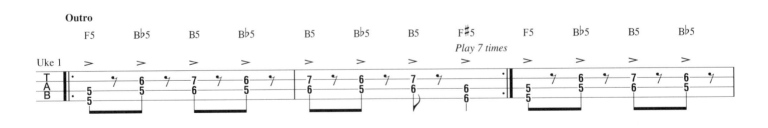

Outro

THE DAY THAT NEVER COMES

Music by Metallica
Lyrics by James Hetfield

Intro
Moderately ♩ = 124

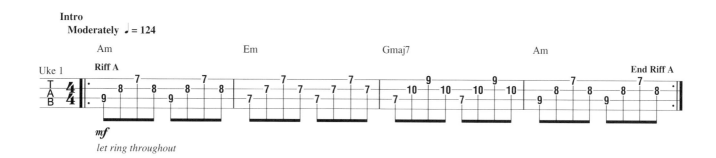

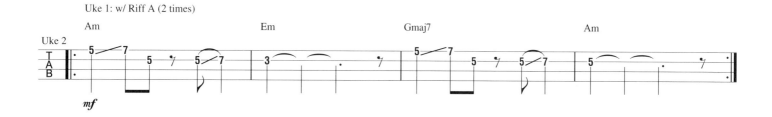

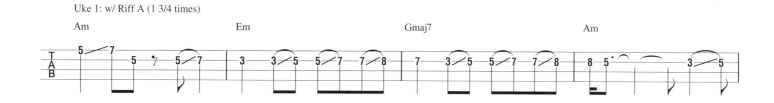

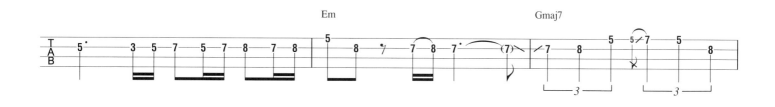

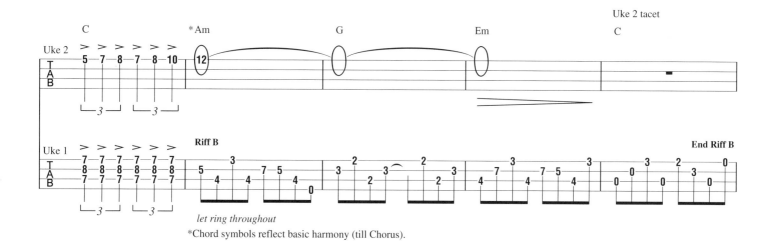

*Chord symbols reflect basic harmony (till Chorus).

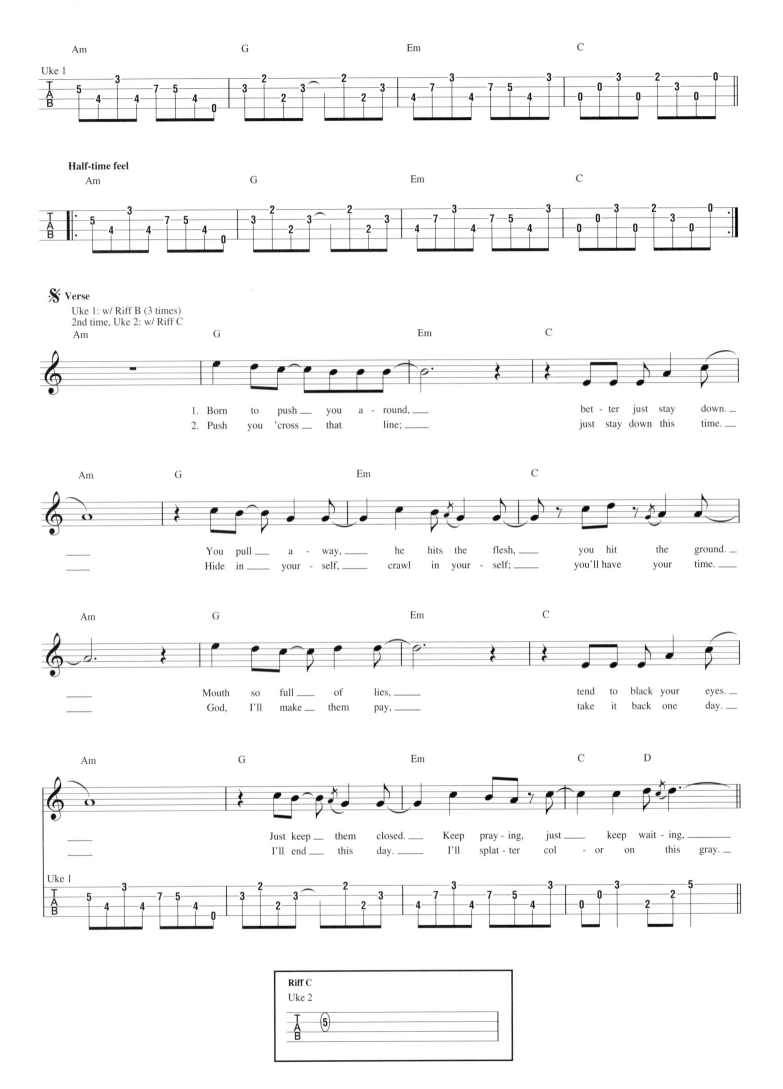

Chorus

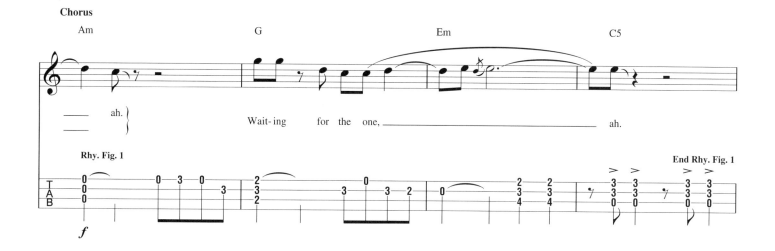

Waiting for the one, ah.

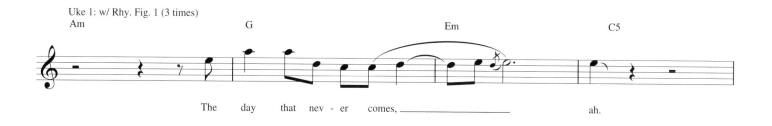

Uke 1: w/ Rhy. Fig. 1 (3 times)

The day that nev-er comes, ah.

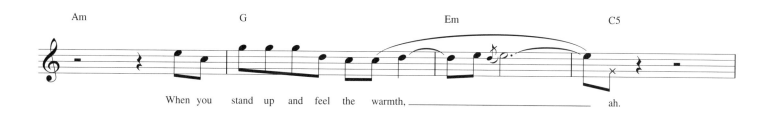

When you stand up and feel the warmth, ah.

End half-time feel

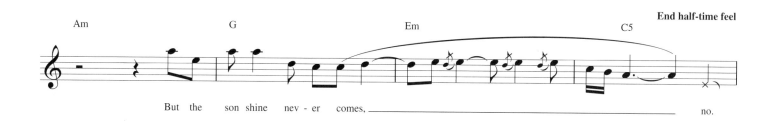

But the son shine nev-er comes, no.

To Coda

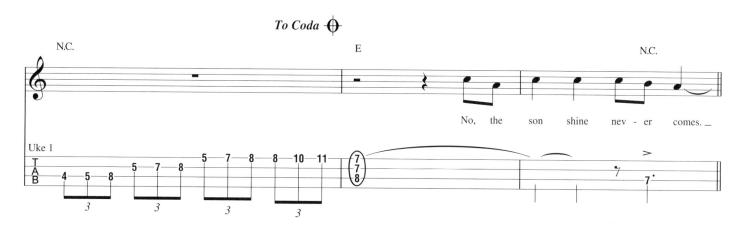

No, the son shine nev-er comes.

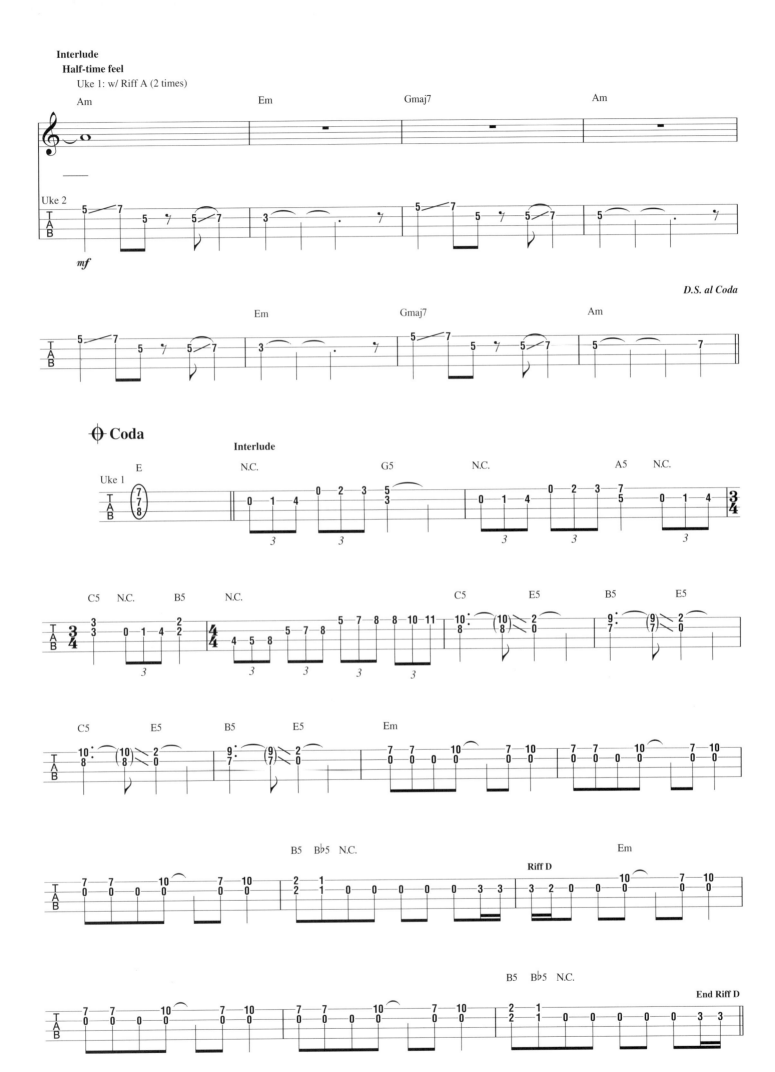

Bridge

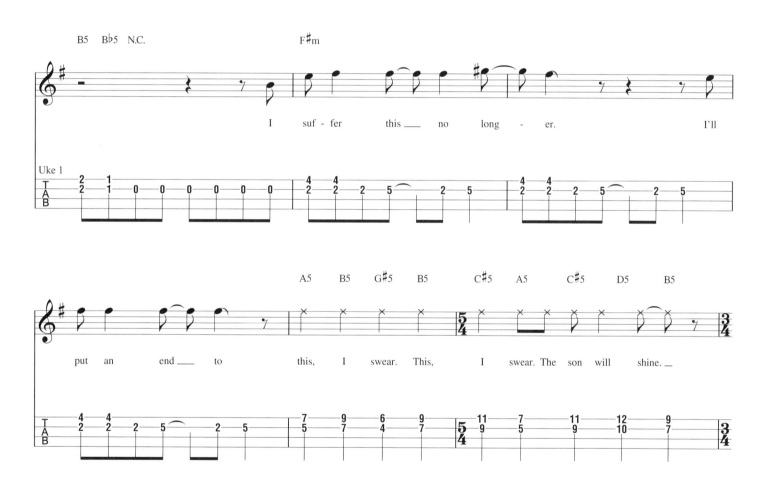

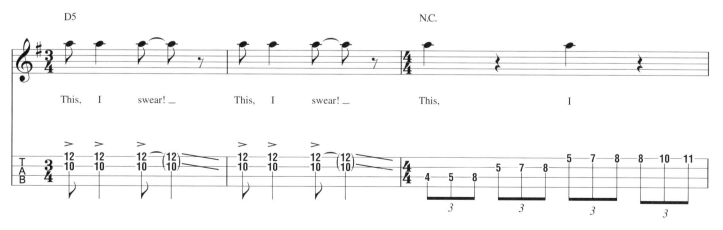

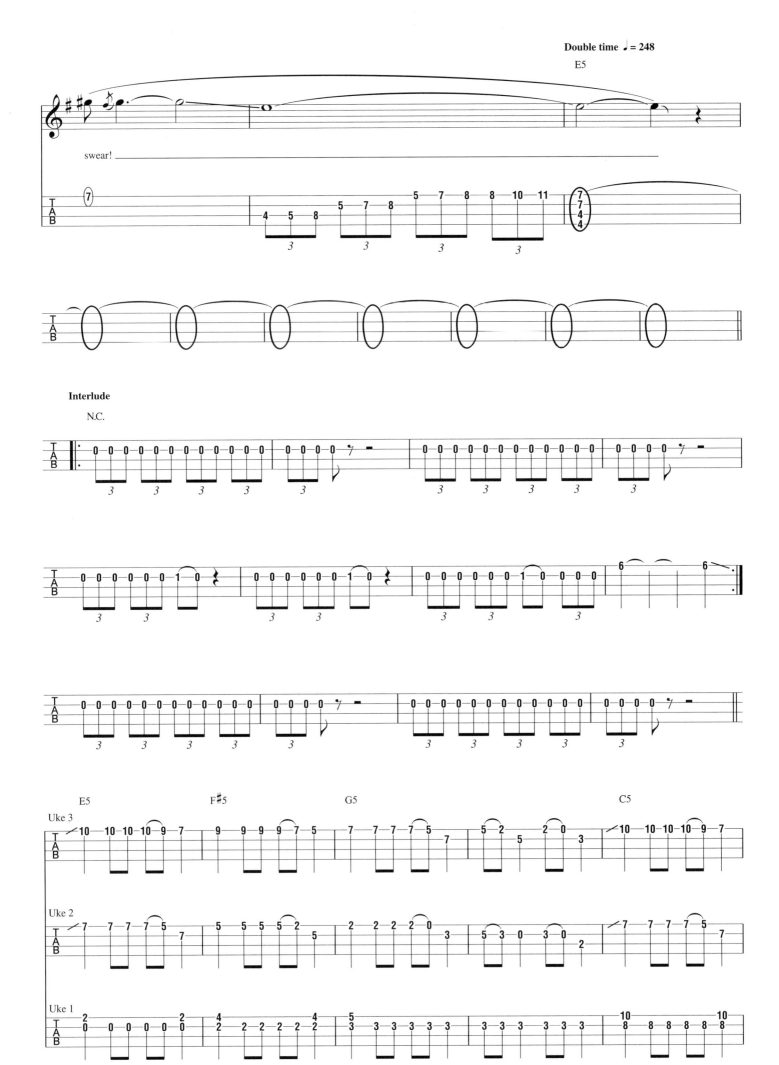

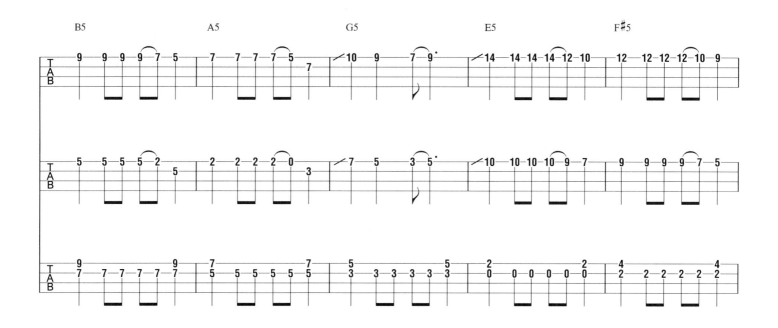

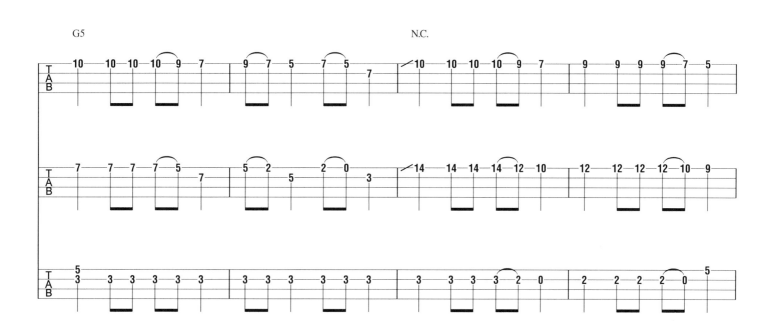

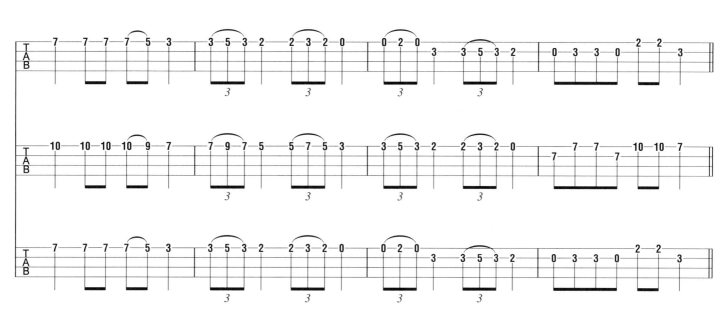

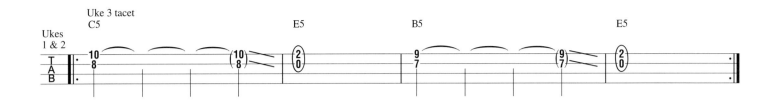

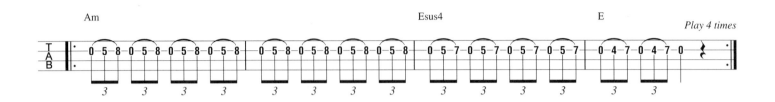

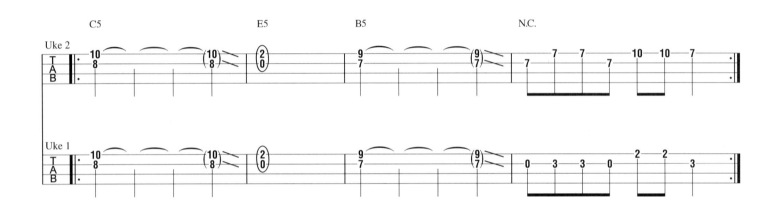

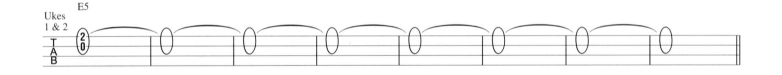

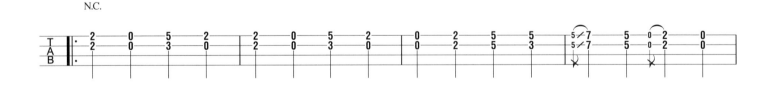

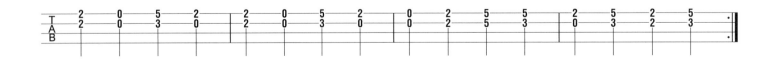

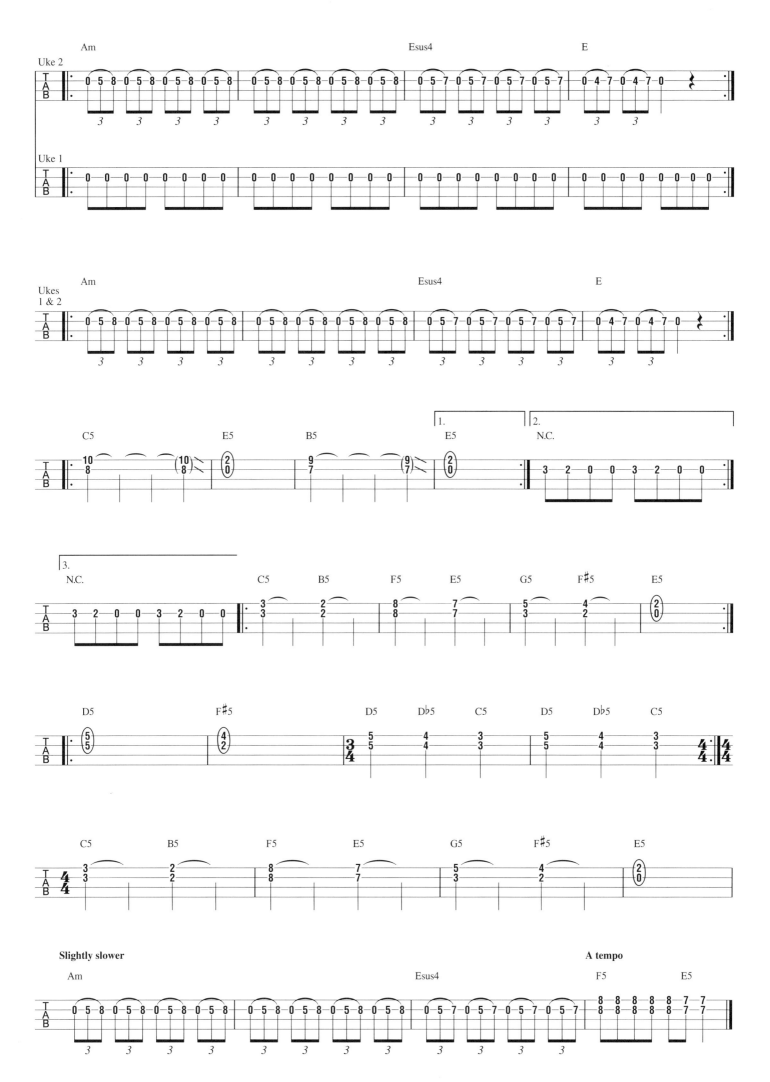

ENTER SANDMAN

Words and Music by
James Hetfield, Lars Ulrich
and Kirk Hammett

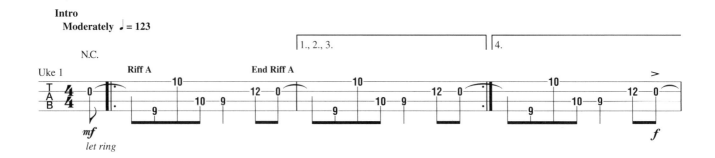

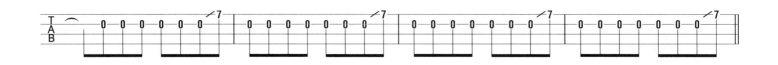

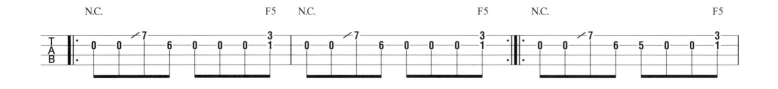

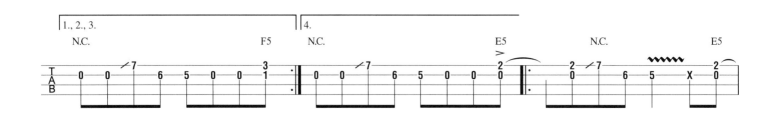

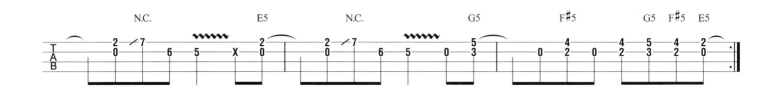

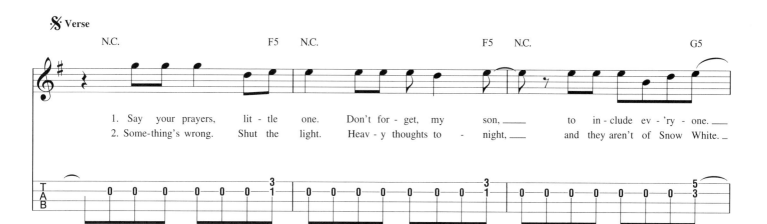

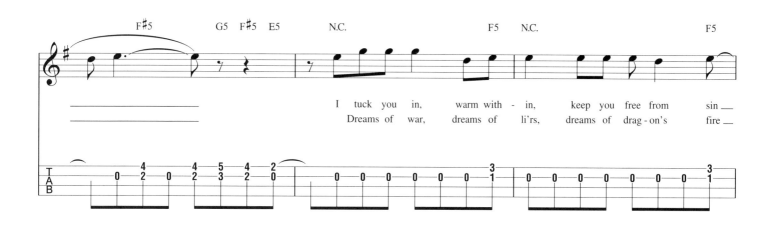

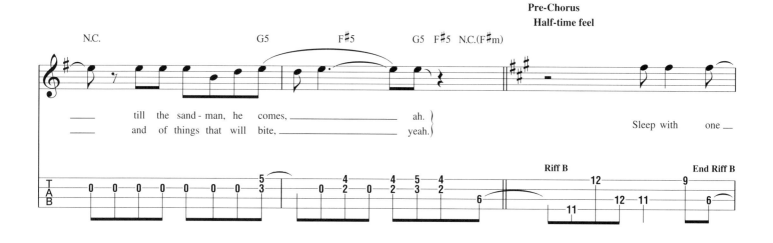

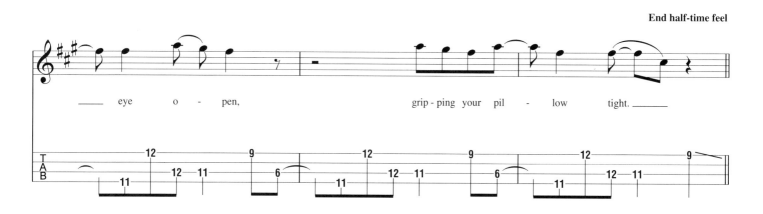

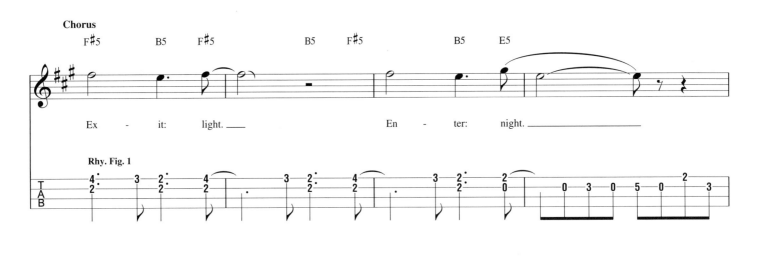

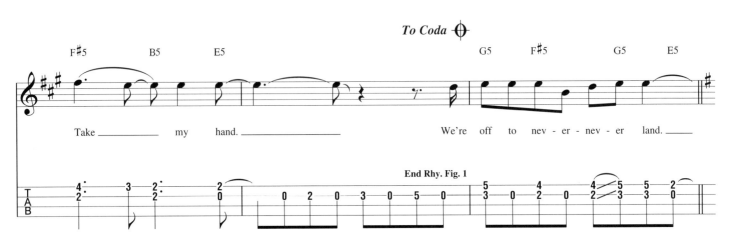

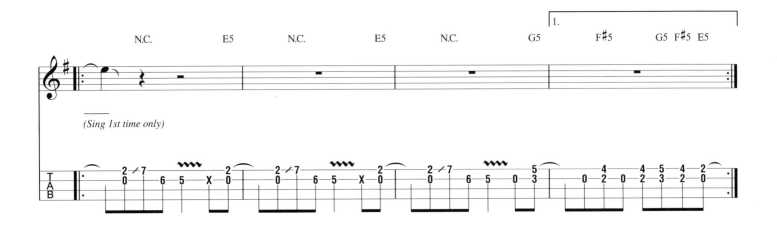

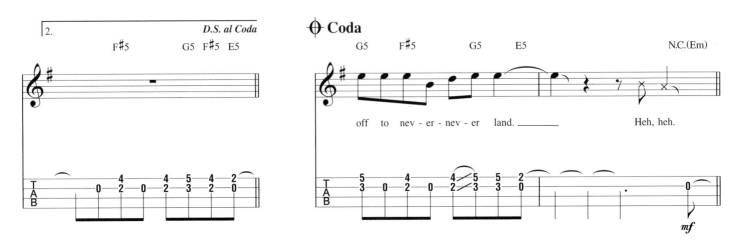

Bridge

(Spoken:) Now I lay me down to sleep.   Pray the Lord my soul to keep.

(Child:) Now I lay me down to sleep.

Pray the Lord my soul to keep.   If I die before I wake,

If I die before I wake,

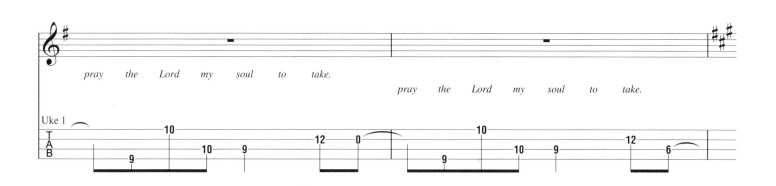

pray the Lord my soul to take.

pray the Lord my soul to take.

Hush, lit - tle ba - by. Don't _____ say a word. _____

And nev - er mind that noise you heard. __   It's just the beasts un - der __

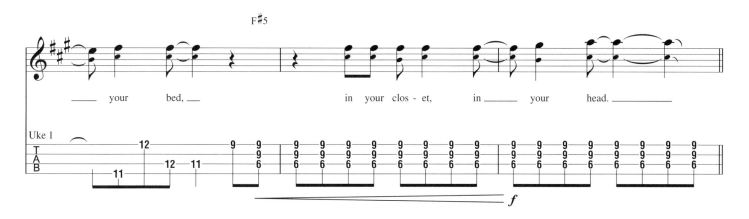

_____ your bed, _____   in your clos - et, in _____ your head. _____

Chorus

Uke 1: w/ Rhy. Fig. 1 (2 times)

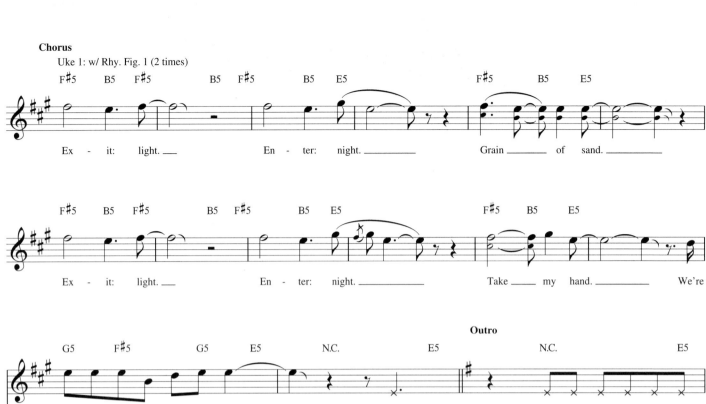

Ex - it: light. ___ En - ter: night. ___ Grain ___ of sand. ___

Ex - it: light. ___ En - ter: night. ___ Take ___ my hand. ___ We're

Outro

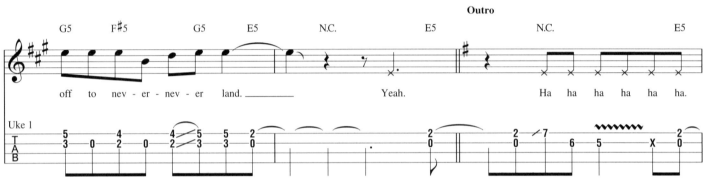

off to nev - er - nev - er land. ___ Yeah. Ha ha ha ha ha ha.

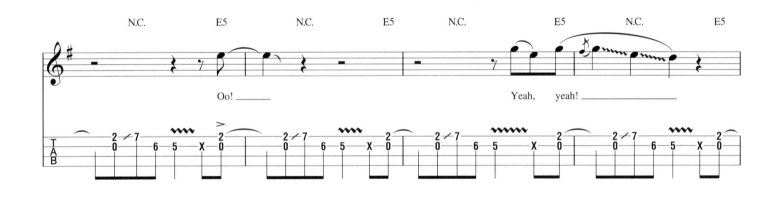

Oo! ___ Yeah, yeah!

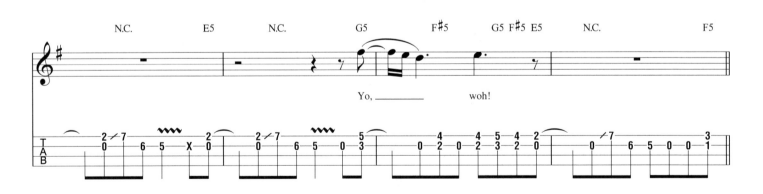

Yo, ___ woh!

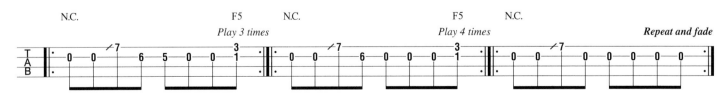

Play 3 times   *Play 4 times*   ***Repeat and fade***

FADE TO BLACK

Words and Music by
James Hetfield, Lars Ulrich,
Cliff Burton and Kirk Hammett

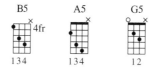

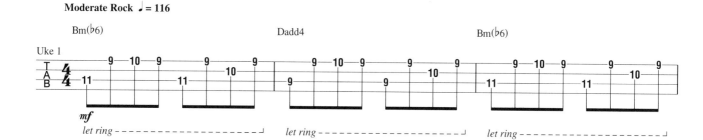

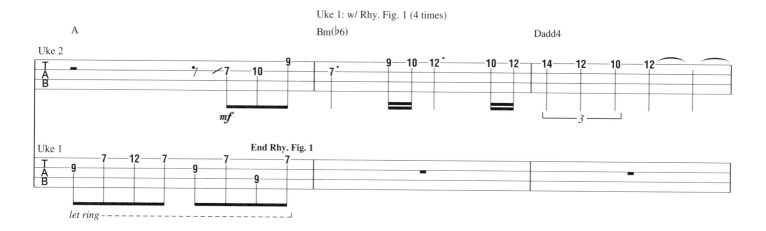

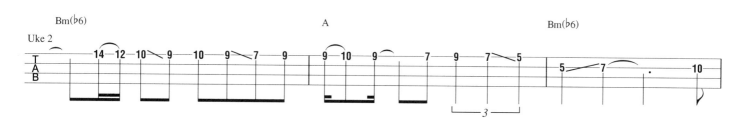

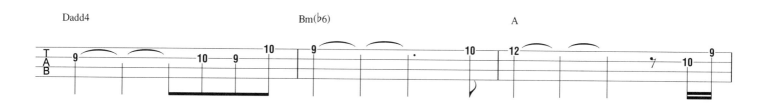

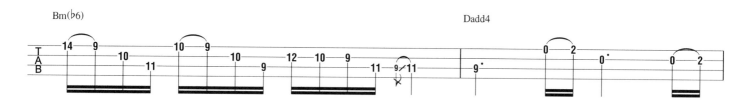

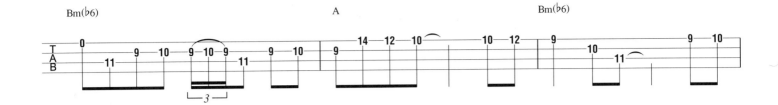

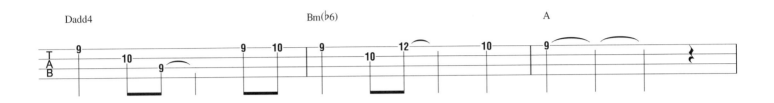

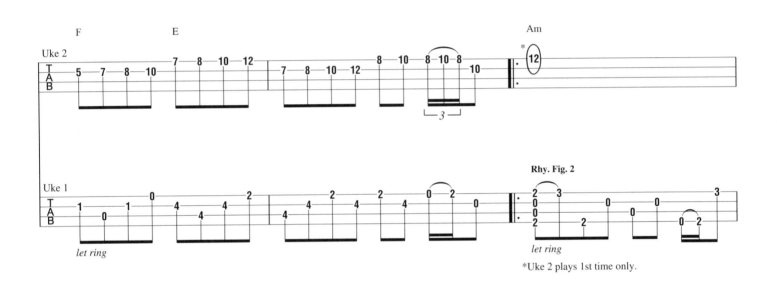

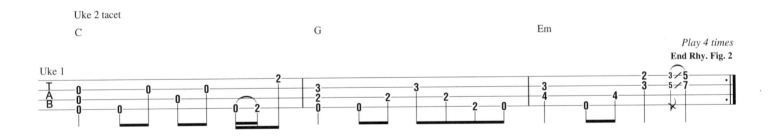

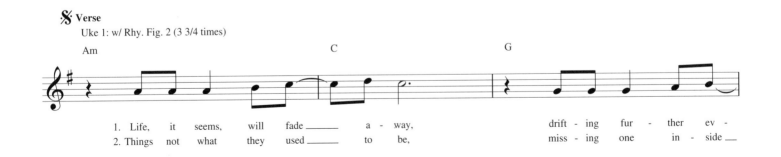

1. Life, it seems, will fade _____ a - way, drift - ing fur - ther ev -
2. Things not what they used _____ to be, miss - ing one in - side _____

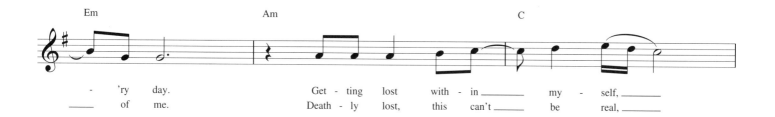

-'ry day.
_____ of me.

Em .... Am C

Get - ting lost with - in _____ my - self, _____
Death - ly lost, this can't _____ be real, _____

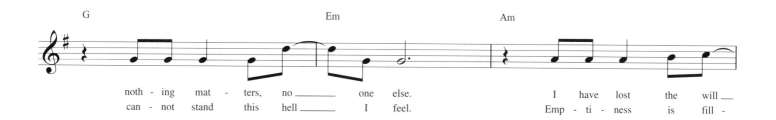

noth - ing mat - ters, no _____ one else.
can - not stand this hell _____ I feel.

G .... Em .... Am

I have lost the will _____
Emp - ti - ness is fill -

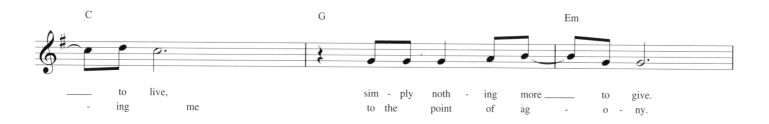

_____ to live,
- ing me

C .... G .... Em

sim - ply noth - ing more _____ to give.
to the point of ag - o - ny.

There is noth - ing more _____ for me; _____
Grow - ing dark - ness tak - ing dawn, _____

Am .... C .... G

need the end to set _____
I was me but now _____

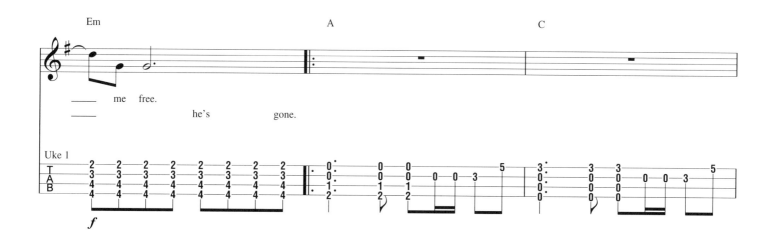

_____ me free.
_____ he's gone.

Em .... A C

Uke 1

f

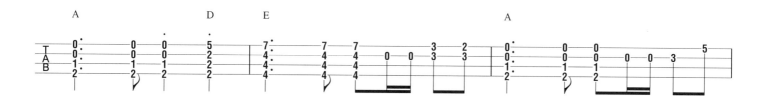

A .... D .... E .... A

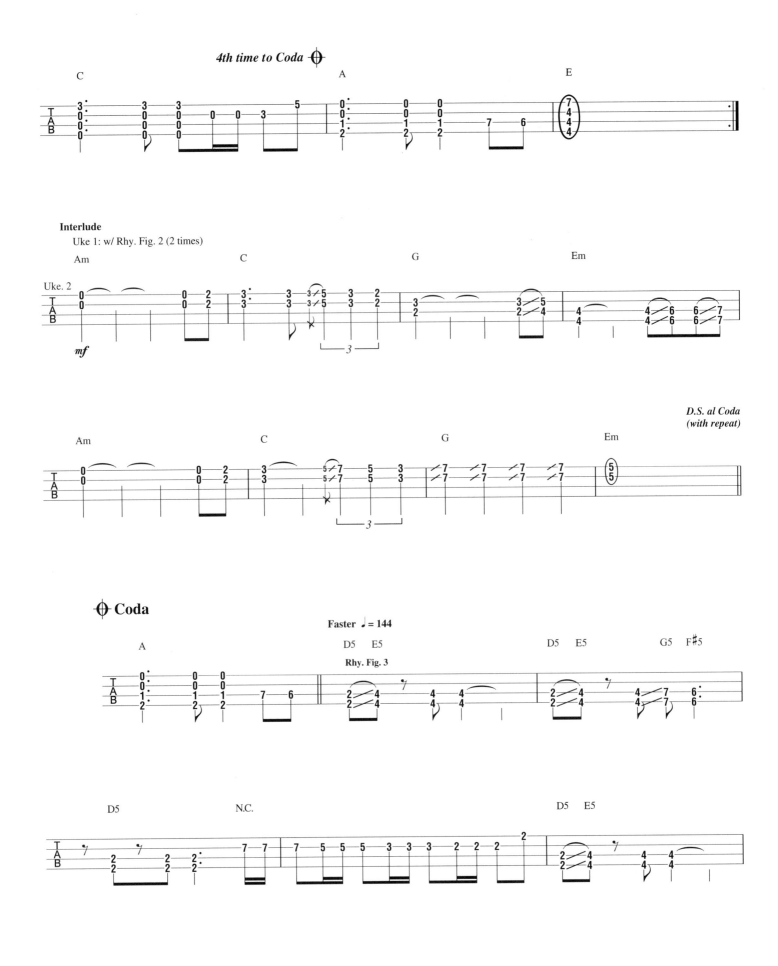

Bridge

Uke 1: w/ Rhy. Fig. 3 (3 times)

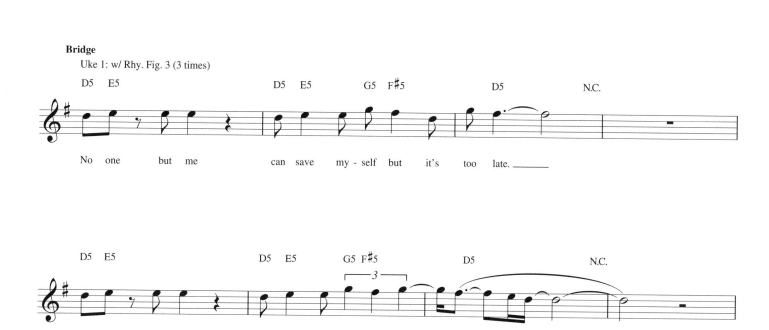

No one but me can save my-self but it's too late. _____

Now I can't think, think why I should e - ven _____ try. _____

Uke 2

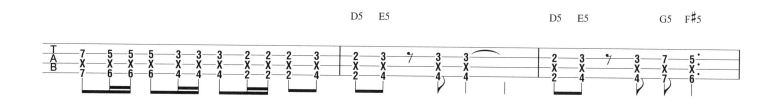

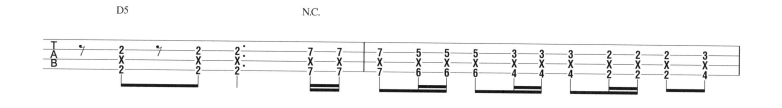

Uke 2 tacet

Yes - ter - day seems as though it nev - er ex - ist - ed. _____

Death greets me warm; now I will just say good - bye. _____

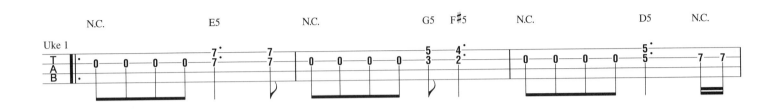

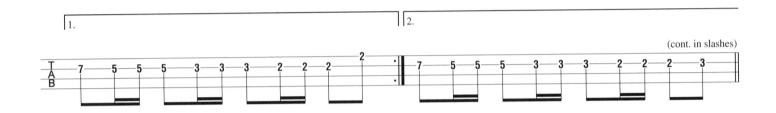

(cont. in slashes)

Outro

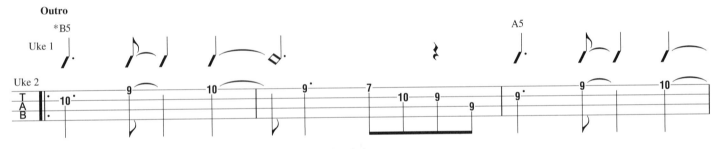

*See top of first page of song for chord diagrams pertaining to rhythm slashes.

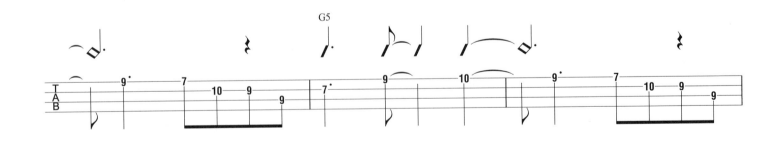

Repeat and fade

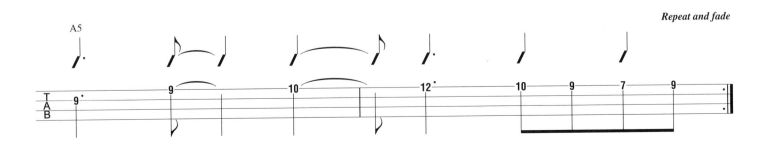

FOR WHOM THE BELL TOLLS

Words and Music by
James Hetfield, Lars Ulrich
and Cliff Burton

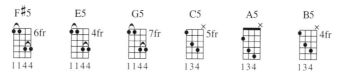

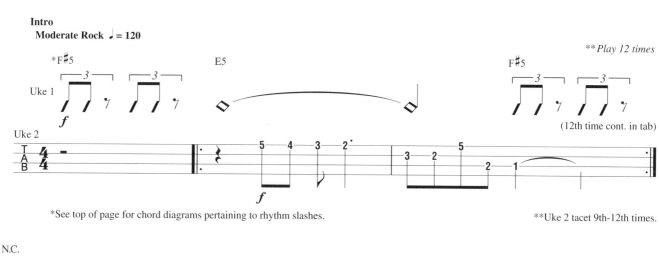

*See top of page for chord diagrams pertaining to rhythm slashes.

**Uke 2 tacet 9th-12th times.

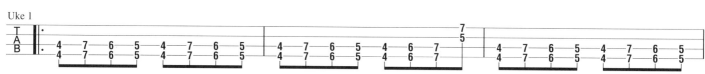

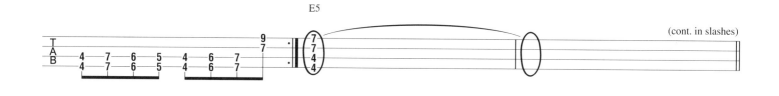

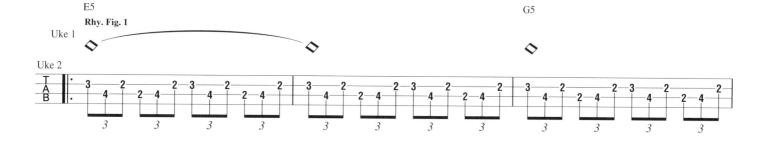

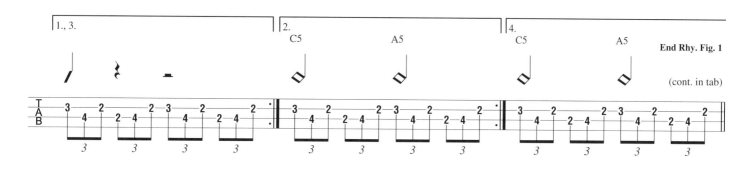

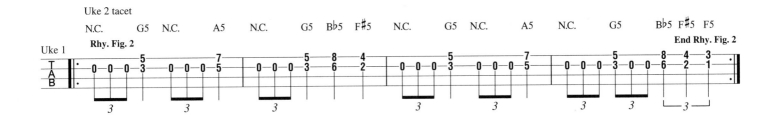

Verse

Uke 1: w/ Rhy. Fig. 1 (2 times)

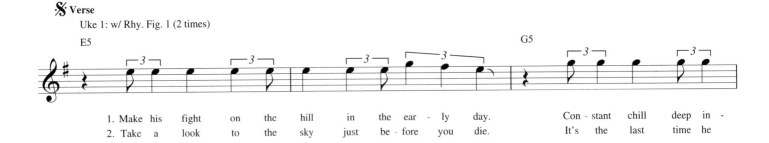

1. Make his fight on the hill in the ear - ly day. Con - stant chill deep in -
2. Take a look to the sky just be - fore you die. It's the last time he

side. Shout - ing gun, on they run through the end - less grey.
will. Black - ened roar, mas - sive roar fills the crum - bling sky.

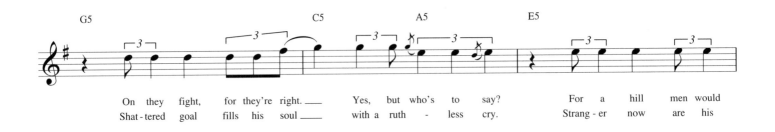

On they fight, for they're right. __ Yes, but who's to say? For a hill men would
Shat - tered goal fills his soul __ with a ruth - less cry. Strang - er now are his

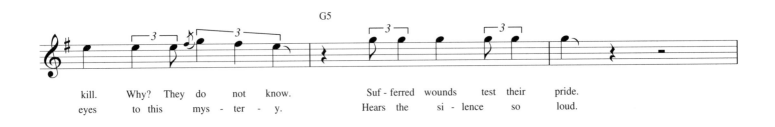

kill. Why? They do not know. Suf - ferred wounds test their pride.
eyes to this mys - ter - y. Hears the si - lence so loud.

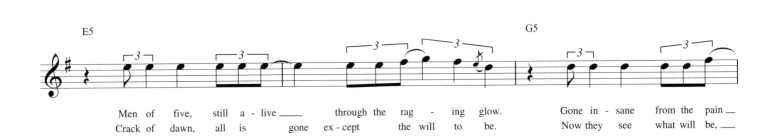

Men of five, still a - live __ through the rag - ing glow. Gone in - sane from the pain __
Crack of dawn, all is gone ex - cept the will to be. Now they see what will be, __

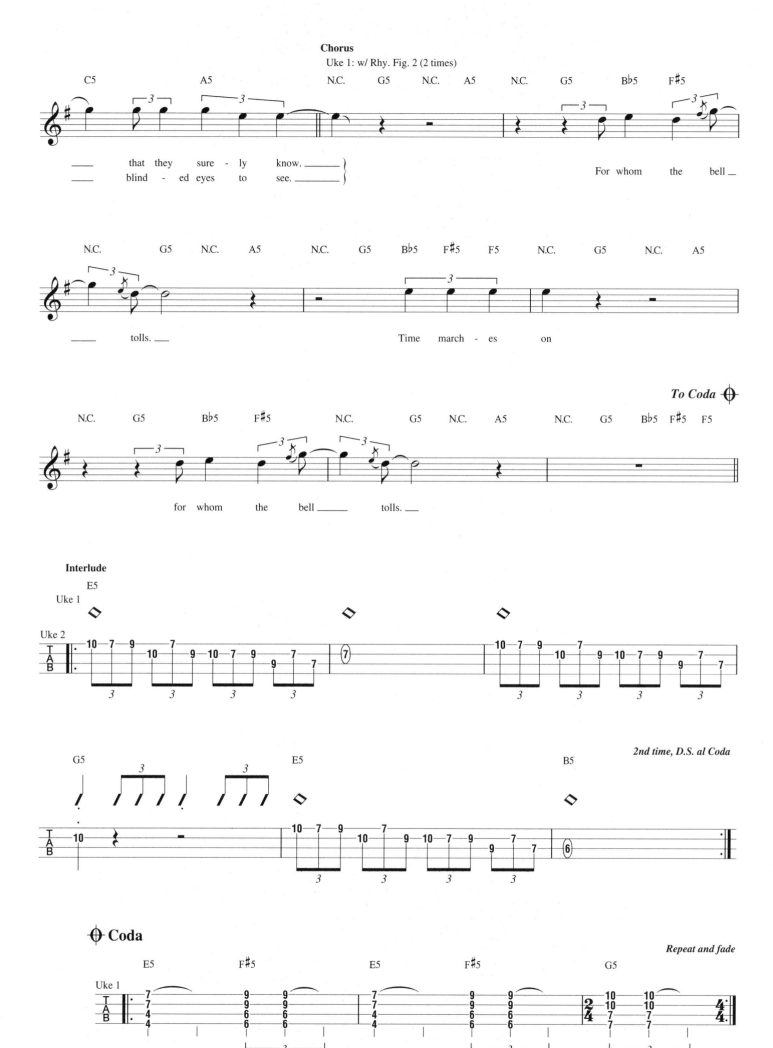

JUMP IN THE FIRE

Words and Music by
James Hetfield, Lars Ulrich
and Dave Mustaine

Intro
Moderate Rock ♩ = 176

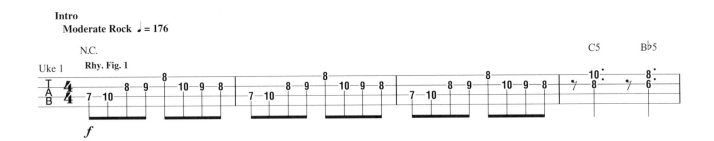

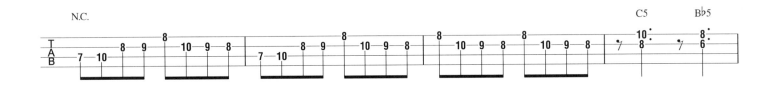

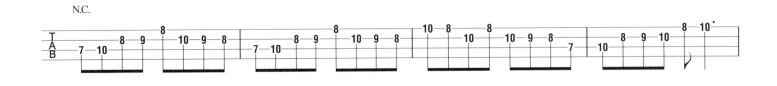

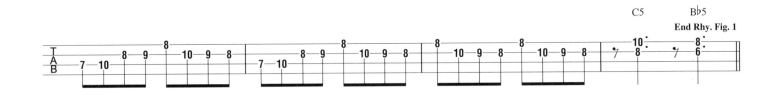

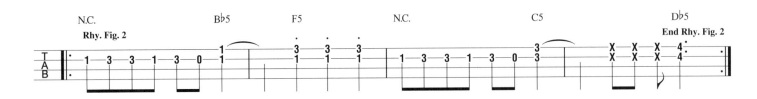

Uke 1: w/ Rhy. Fig. 1

Jump in the fi -

- re! So come on! ___

___ Jump in the fi -

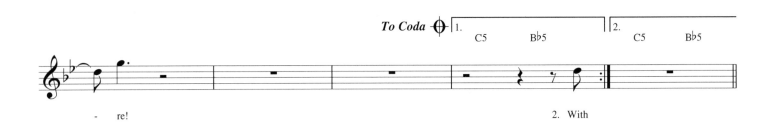

- re! 2. With

Interlude

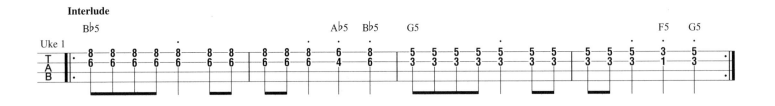

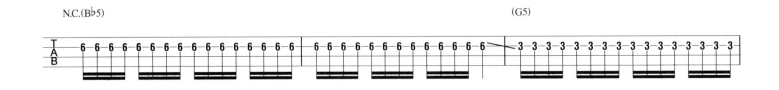

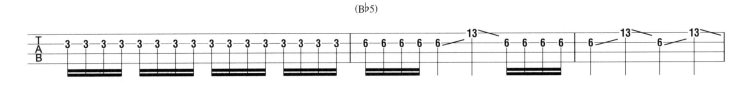

(G5)

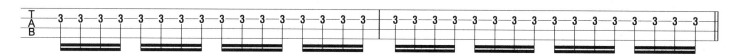

⊕ Coda

Uke 1: w/ Rhy. Fig. 1

So come on! _____

Jump in the fi - re!   So come on! _

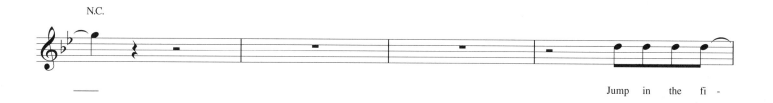

_____   Jump in the fi -

- re!   Come on,   jump, _ ba - by now! _

Repeat and fade

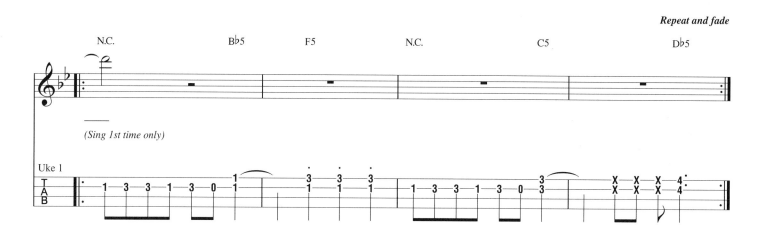

(Sing 1st time only)

KING NOTHING

Words and Music by
James Hetfield, Lars Ulrich
and Kirk Hammett

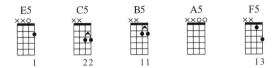

E5 C5 B5 A5 F5

Tune down 1/2 step:
(low to high) G♭-C♭-E♭-A♭

Intro
Moderately ♩ = 120

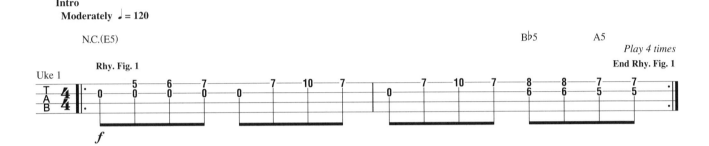

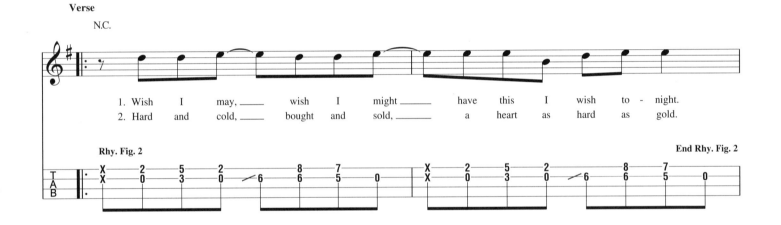

1. Wish I may, ____ wish I might ____ have this I wish to-night.
2. Hard and cold, ____ bought and sold, ____ a heart as hard as gold.

Uke 1: w/ Rhy. Fig. 2 (3 times)

Are you sat - is - fied? ____   Dig for gold, ____ dig for fame.
Yeah, are you sat - is - fied? ____   Wish I might, ____ wish I may. ____

____ You dig to make your name.   Are you pac - i - fied? ____
____ You wish your life a - way.   Are you pac - i - fied? ____

Pre-Chorus
Half-time feel

*See top of first page of song for chord diagrams pertaining to rhythm slashes.

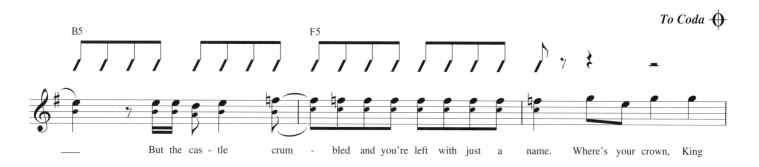

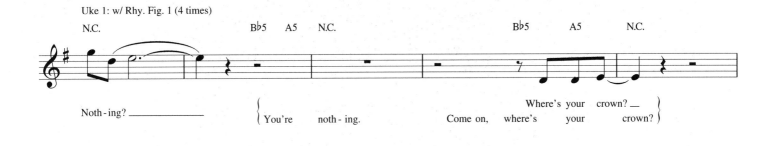

Uke 1: w/ Rhy. Fig. 1 (4 times)

Noth - ing? _____ You're noth - ing. Where's your crown? __ Come on, where's your crown?

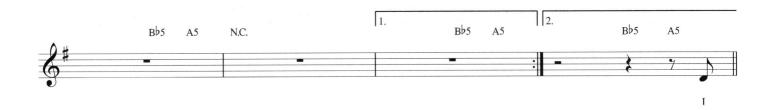

I

Bridge

wish I may, ____ I wish I might ____

Uke 1 **Riff A** **End Riff A**

mf

Uke 1: w/ Riff A (7 times)

have this wish ____ I wish ____ to - night. ____ I want that star, ____ I

want it now. ____ I want it all ____ and I don't ____ care ____ how. ____

Care - ful ____ what ____ you ____ wish, ____ care - ful ____ what ____

you say. Care - ful what you ___ wish, ___ you ___ may ___ re - gret ___ it. Care - ful

D.S. al Coda

what you _____ wish, _____ you just _____ might get _____ it. _____

⊕ Coda

Uke 1: w/ Rhy. Fig. 1

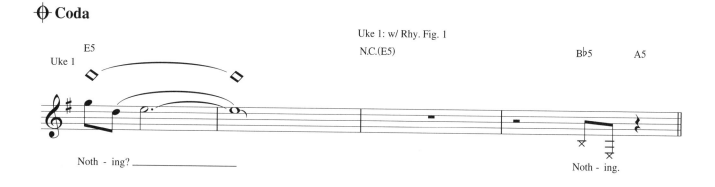

Noth - ing? _____ Noth - ing.

Outro

Uke 1: w/ Rhy. Fig. 1 (4 times)

Mm, ___ no, ___ you're just noth - ing. ___ Where's your crown, __ King

Noth - ing? ___ No, _____ you're just noth - ing. ___ Ab - so -

Free time

lute - ly noth - ing. Off to nev - er - nev - er land. _____

MASTER OF PUPPETS

Words and Music by
James Hetfield, Lars Ulrich,
Kirk Hammett and Cliff Burton

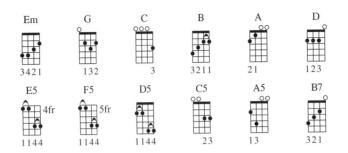

Intro
Fast Rock ♩ = 220

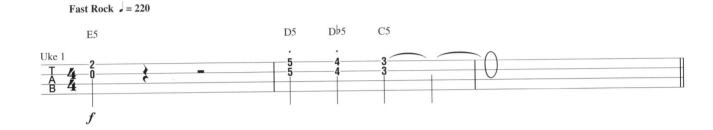

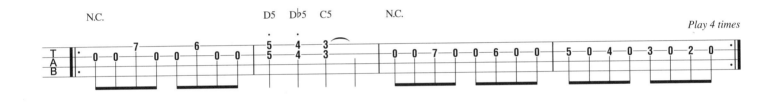

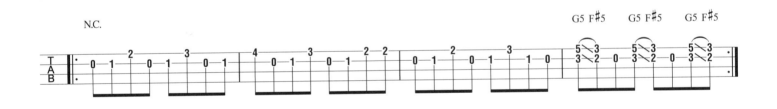

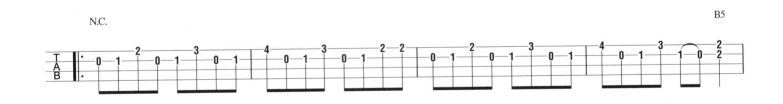

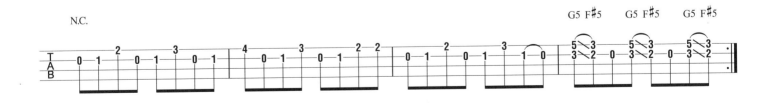

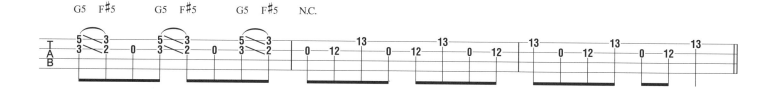

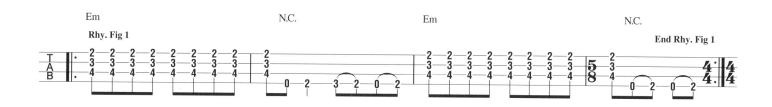

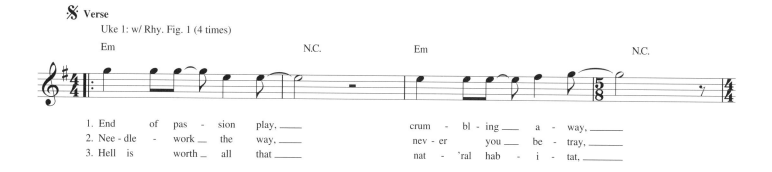

%. Verse

Uke 1: w/ Rhy. Fig. 1 (4 times)

1. End of pas - sion play, _____ crum - bl - ing _____ a - way, _____
2. Nee - dle - work _ the way, _____ nev - er you _ be - tray, _____
3. Hell is worth _ all that _____ nat - 'ral hab - i - tat, _____

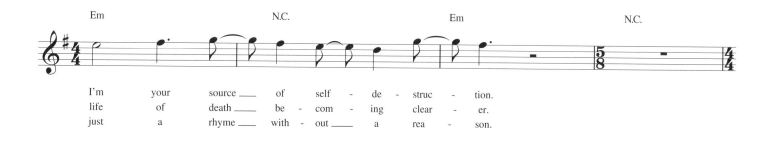

I'm your source _____ of self - de - struc - tion.
life of death _____ be - com - ing clear - er.
just a rhyme _____ with - out _____ a rea - son.

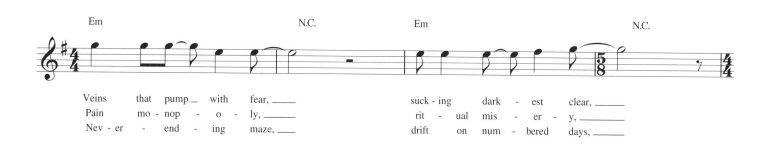

Veins that pump _ with fear, _____ suck - ing dark - est clear, _____
Pain mo - nop - o - ly, _____ rit - ual mis - er - y, _____
Nev - er - end - ing maze, _____ drift on num - bered days, _____

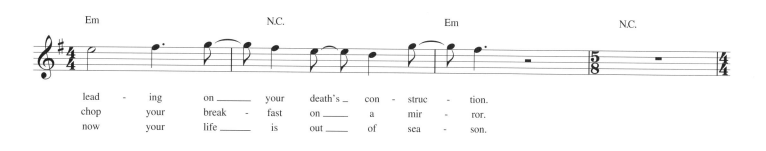

lead - ing on _____ your death's _ con - struc - tion.
chop your break - fast on _____ a mir - ror.
now your life _____ is out _ of sea - son.

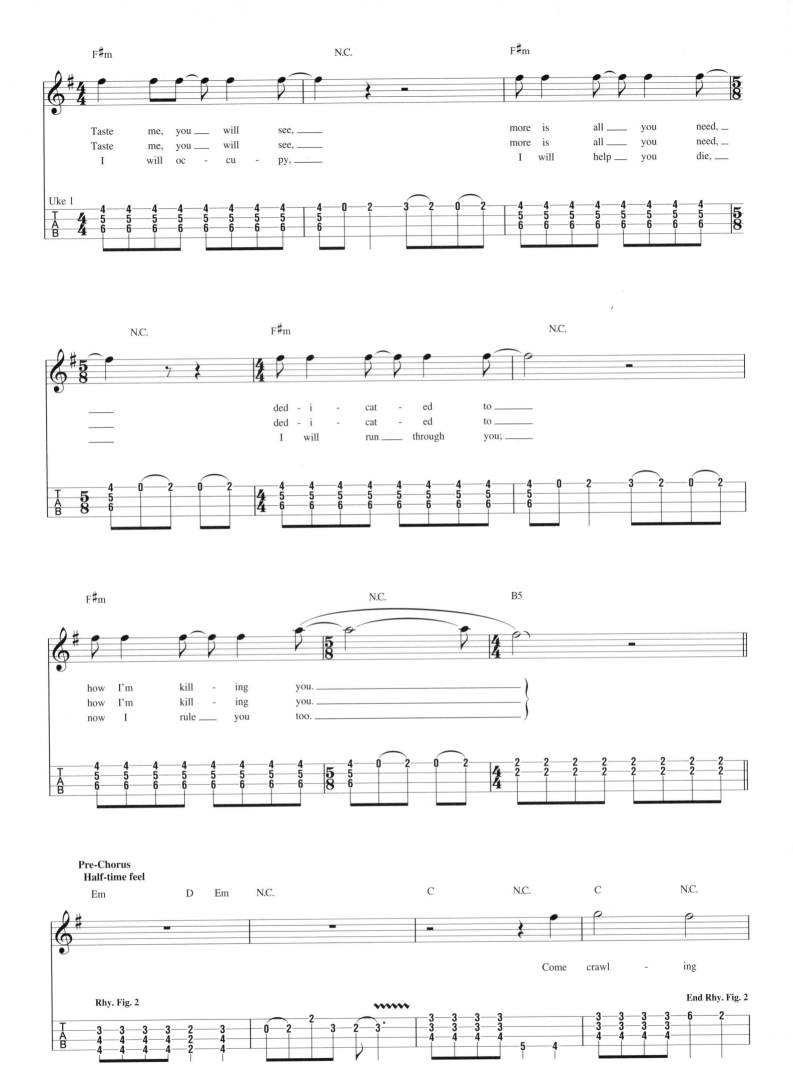

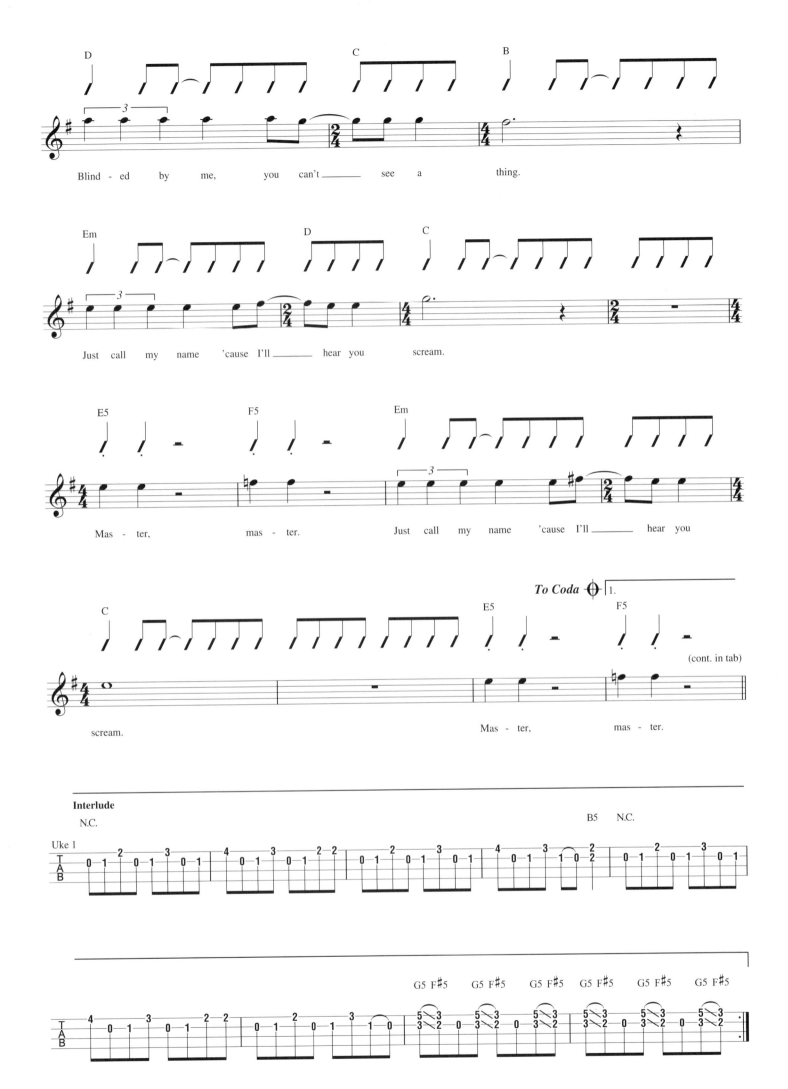

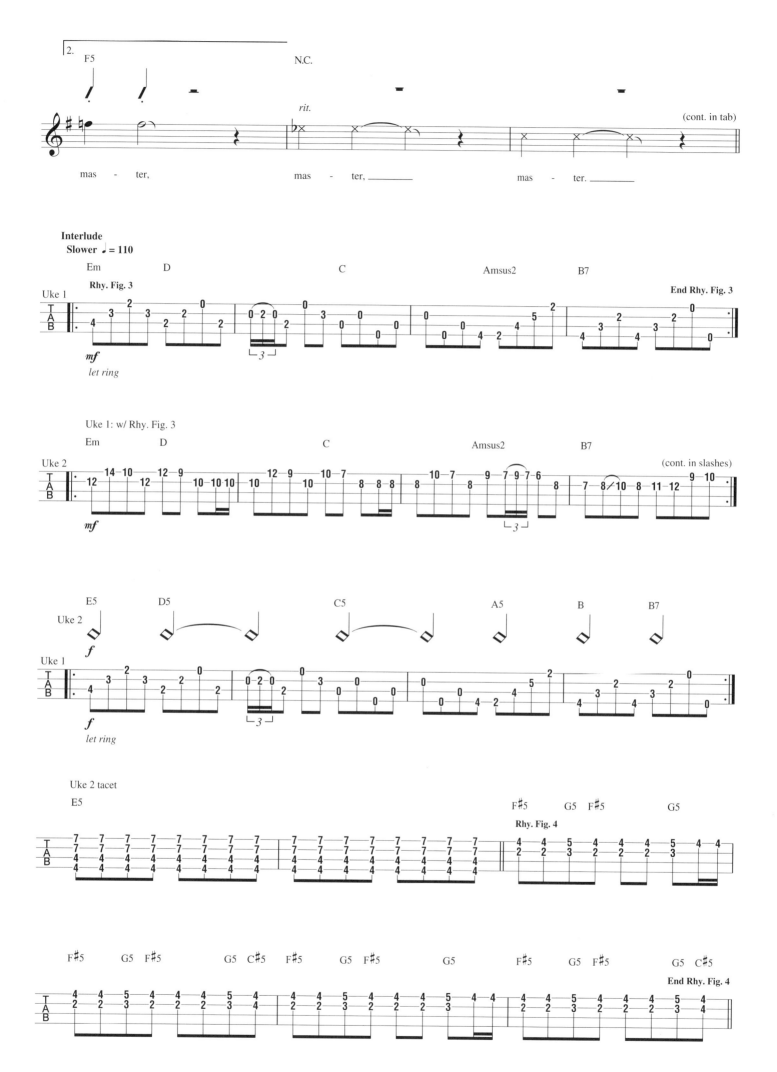

Bridge

Uke 1: w/ Rhy. Fig. 4 (2 times)

Mas - ter, mas - ter, where's the dreams that I've __ been af - ter? Mas - ter, mas - ter,

prom - ised on - ly lies. __ Laugh - ter, laugh - ter, all I hear __ or see __ is laugh - ter.

Laugh - ter, laugh - ter, laugh - ing at _____ my cries. __

Faster ♩ = 220

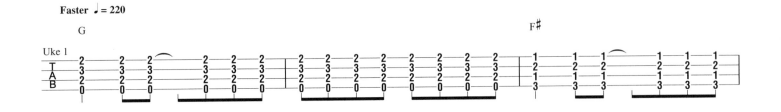

Interlude

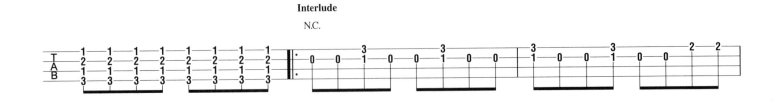

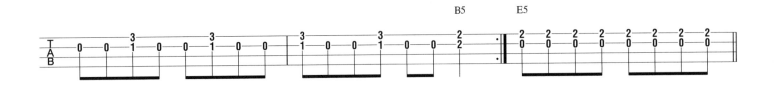

44

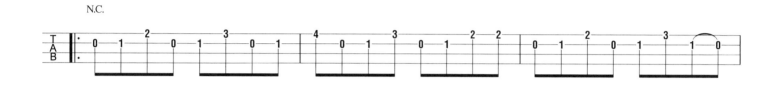

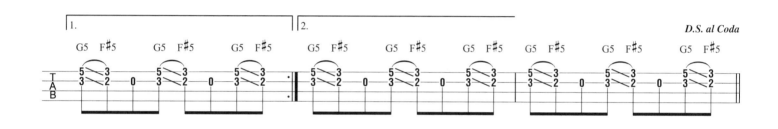

Coda

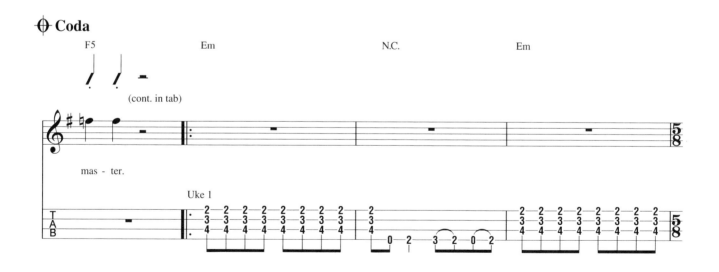

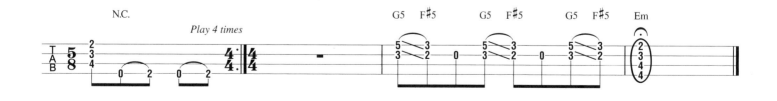

THE MEMORY REMAINS

Words and Music by
James Hetfield and Lars Ulrich

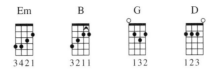

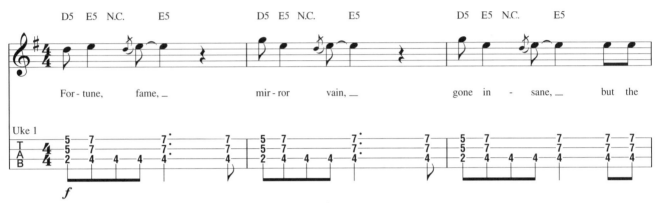

Tune down 1/2 step:
(low to high) G♭-C♭-E♭-A♭

Intro
Moderate Rock ♩ = 148

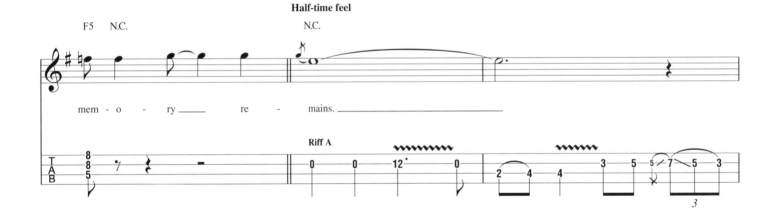

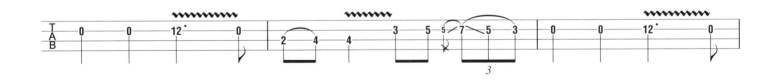

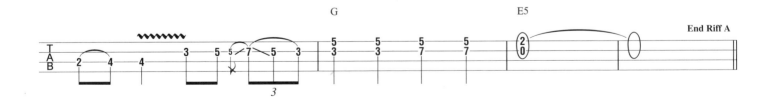

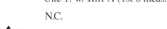

Verse

Uke 1: w/ Riff A (1st 6 meas.)

1. Heav - y rings ___ on fin - gers wave, ___ an - oth - er star ___
2. Heav - y rings ___ hold cig - a - rettes ___ up to lips ___

___ de - nies ___ the grave. ___ See the no - where crowd ___ cry the
___ that time ___ for - gets ___ while the Hol - ly - wood ___ sun

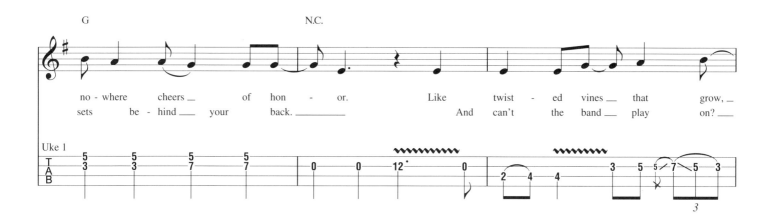

no - where cheers ___ of hon - or. Like twist - ed vines ___ that grow, ___
sets be - hind ___ your back. ___ And can't the band ___ play on? ___

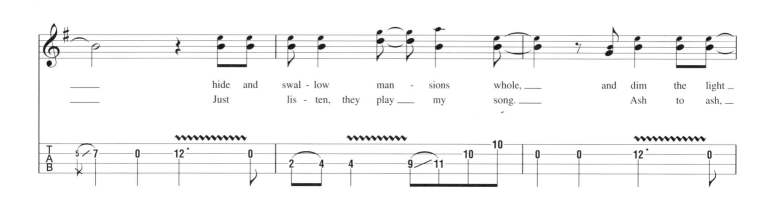

___ hide and swal - low man - sions whole, ___ and dim the light ___
Just lis - ten, they play ___ my song. ___ Ash to ash, ___

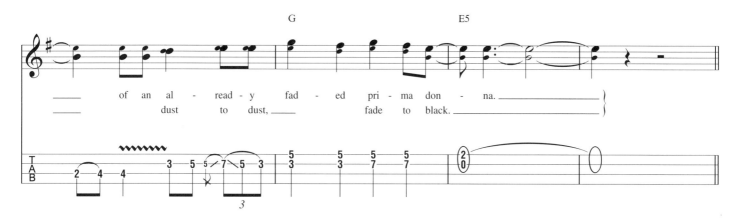

___ of an al - read - y fad - ed pri - ma don - na. ___ }
___ dust to dust, ___ fade to black. ___ }

%S Bridge

*Em

Rhy. Fig. 2

B

G

D

B

End Rhy. Fig. 2

Uke 1

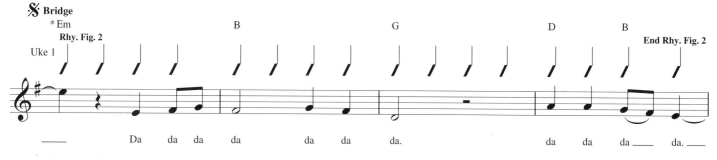

_____ Da da da da da da da. da da da _____ da.

*See top of first page of song for chord diagrams pertaining to rhythm slashes.

Uke 1: w/ Rhy. Fig. 2 (3 times)

Em   B   G   D   B

_____ Da da da da da da da, da da da _____ da

Em   B   G   D   B

da. Da da da da da da da, da da da _____ da. _____

To Coda ⊕

Em   B   G   D   B

_____ Da da da da da da da, da da da _____ da _____

Chorus

Uke 1: w/ Rhy. Fig. 1 (2 times)

D5 E5 N.C.   E5   D5 E5 N.C.   E5   D5 E5 N.C.   E5   D5 G5   D5 G5

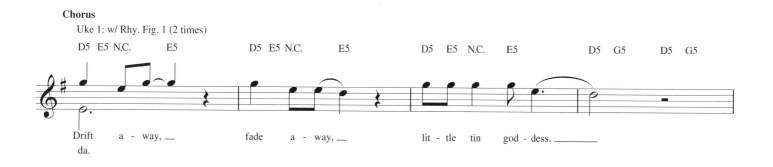

Drift a - way, _____ fade a - way, _____ lit - tle tin god - dess. _____
da.

D5 E5 N.C.   E5   D5 E5 N.C.   E5   D5 E5 N.C.   E5   D5 G5   D5 G5

Ash to ash, _____ dust to dust, fade to black. _____

NOTHING ELSE MATTERS

Words and Music by
James Hetfield and Lars Ulrich

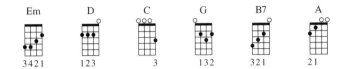

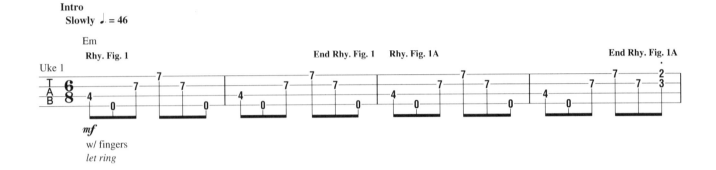

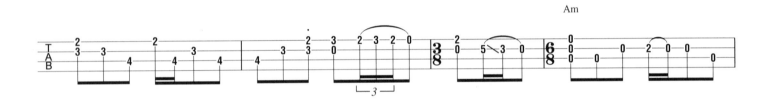

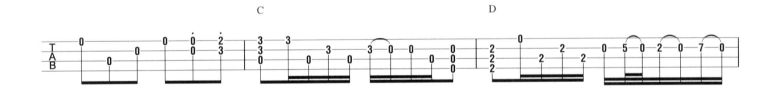

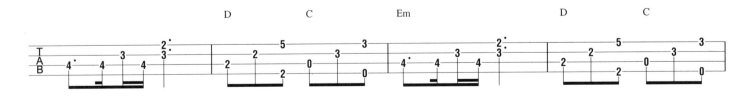

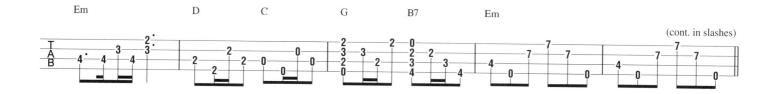

(cont. in slashes)

%. Verse

*Em
Rhy. Fig. 2

Uke 1

1., 4. So close no mat-ter how __ far. _____
2. Nev-er o-pened my -self this way. __
3. Trust I seek and I find in you. __

Could-n't be much more __
Life is ours, we live it
Ev-'ry day for us __

*See top of first page of song for chord diagrams pertaining to rhythm slashes.

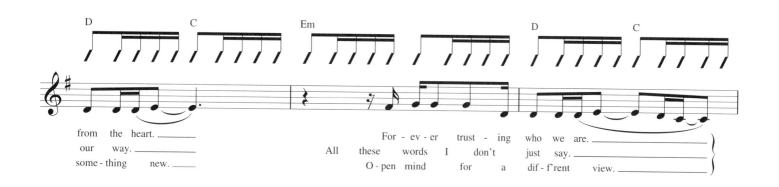

from the heart. _____
our way. _____
some-thing new. _____

For-ev-er trust-ing who we are. _____
All these words I don't just say. _____
O-pen mind for a dif-f'rent view. _____

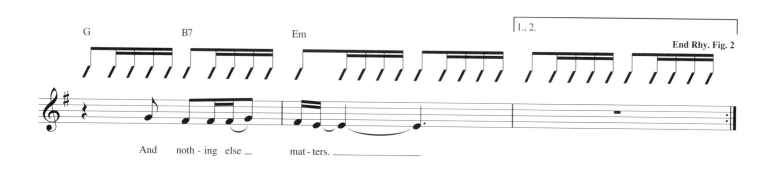

And noth-ing else __ mat-ters. _____

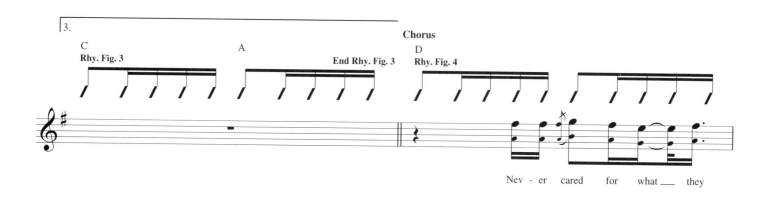

Nev-er cared for what __ they

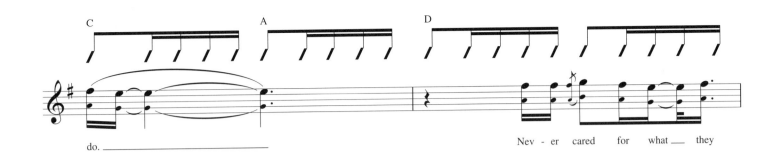

C   A   D

do. _____

Nev - er cared for what ___ they

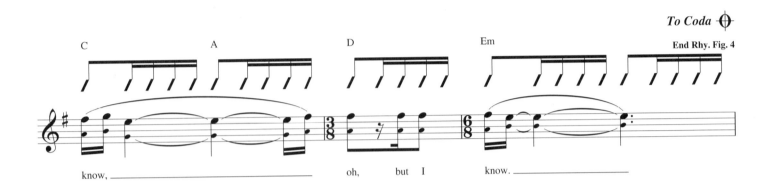

C   A   D   Em

To Coda ⊕

End Rhy. Fig. 4

know, _____

oh, but I know. _____

D.S. al Coda
(take 3rd ending)

⊕ **Coda**

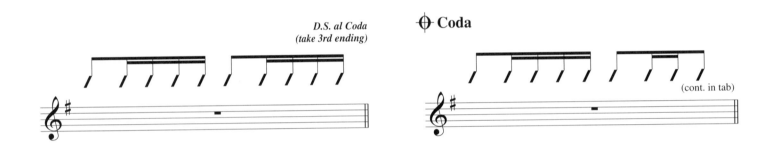

(cont. in tab)

Interlude

N.C.(Em)   Am

C   Dsus2

1.   2.

Em

Verse

1st time, Uke 1: w/ Rhy. Fig. 2
2nd time, Uke 1: w/ Rhy. Fig. 2 (1st 8 meas.)

5. I nev-er o-pened my-self this way. _____ Life is ours; we live it
6. Trust I seek and I find in you. _____ Ev-'ry day for us

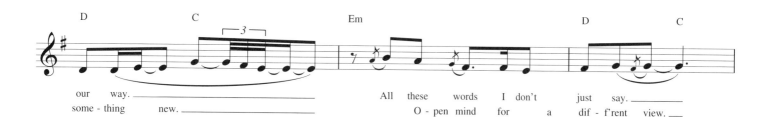

our way. _____ All these words I don't just say. _____
some-thing new. _____ O-pen mind for a dif-f'rent view. __

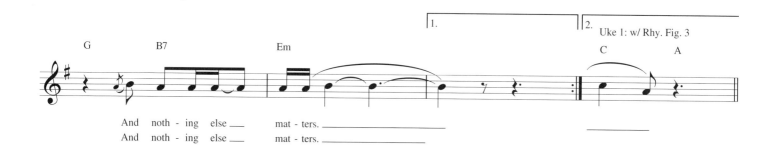

1.
2. Uke 1: w/ Rhy. Fig. 3

And noth-ing else _____ mat-ters. _____
And noth-ing else _____ mat-ters. _____

Chorus

Uke 1: w/ Rhy. Fig. 4 (1st 4 meas.)

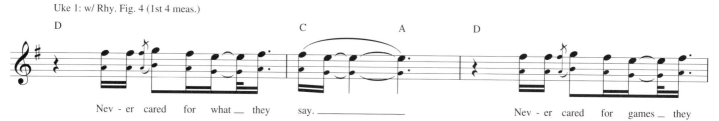

Nev-er cared for what _____ they say. _____ Nev-er cared for games _____ they

Uke 1: w/ Rhy. Fig. 4

play. _____ Nev-er cared for what _____ they do. _____ Nev-er cared for what _____ they

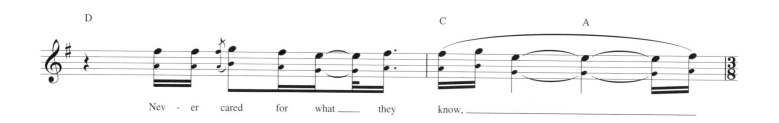

Nev-er cared for what _____ they know, _____

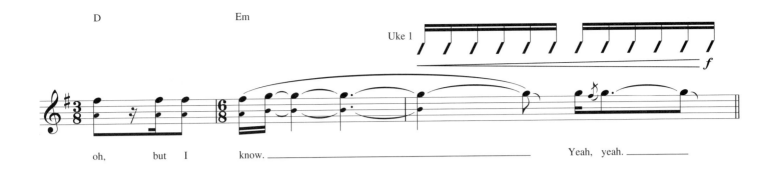

oh,   but   I   know. _____ Yeah,   yeah. _____

Solo

Uke 1: w/ Rhy. Fig. 2 (1st 7 meas.)

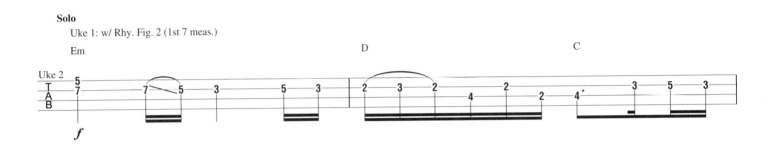

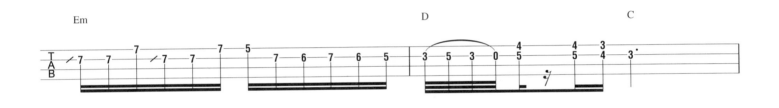

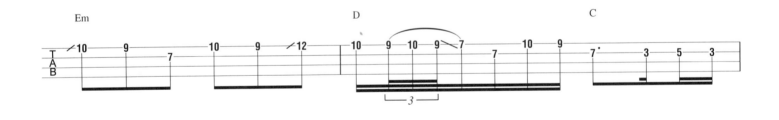

Uke 1: w/ Rhy. Fig. 1 (2 times)

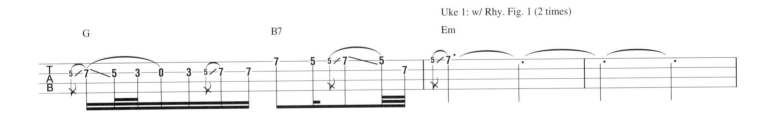

Verse

Uke 1: w/ Rhy. Fig. 2 (1st 7 meas.)
Uke 2 tacet

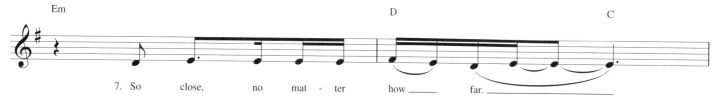

7. So close, no mat - ter how _____ far. _____

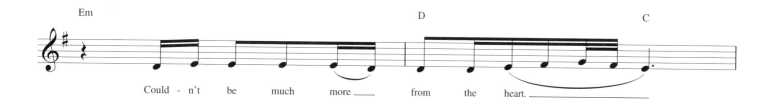

Could - n't be much more _____ from the heart. _____

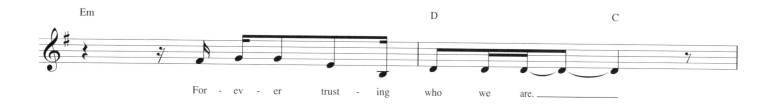

For - ev - er trust - ing who we are. _____

Uke 1: w/ Rhy. Fig. 1A

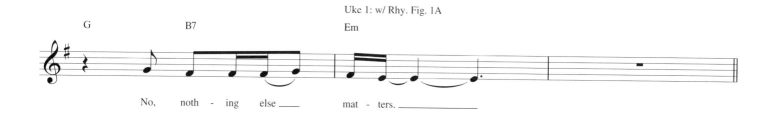

No, noth - ing else _____ mat - ters. _____

Outro

Em

Uke 1

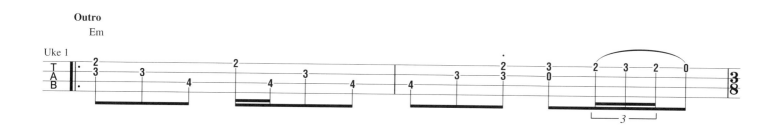

Repeat and fade

ONE

Words and Music by
James Hetfield and Lars Ulrich

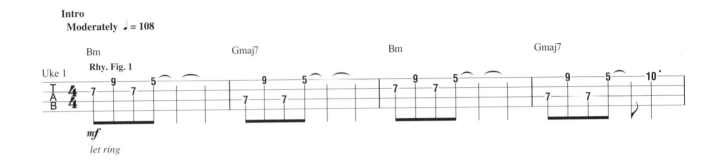

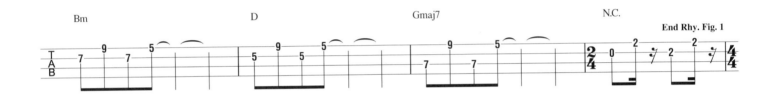

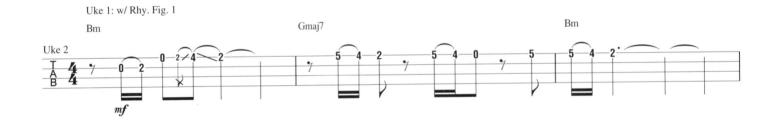

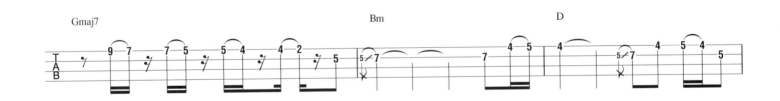

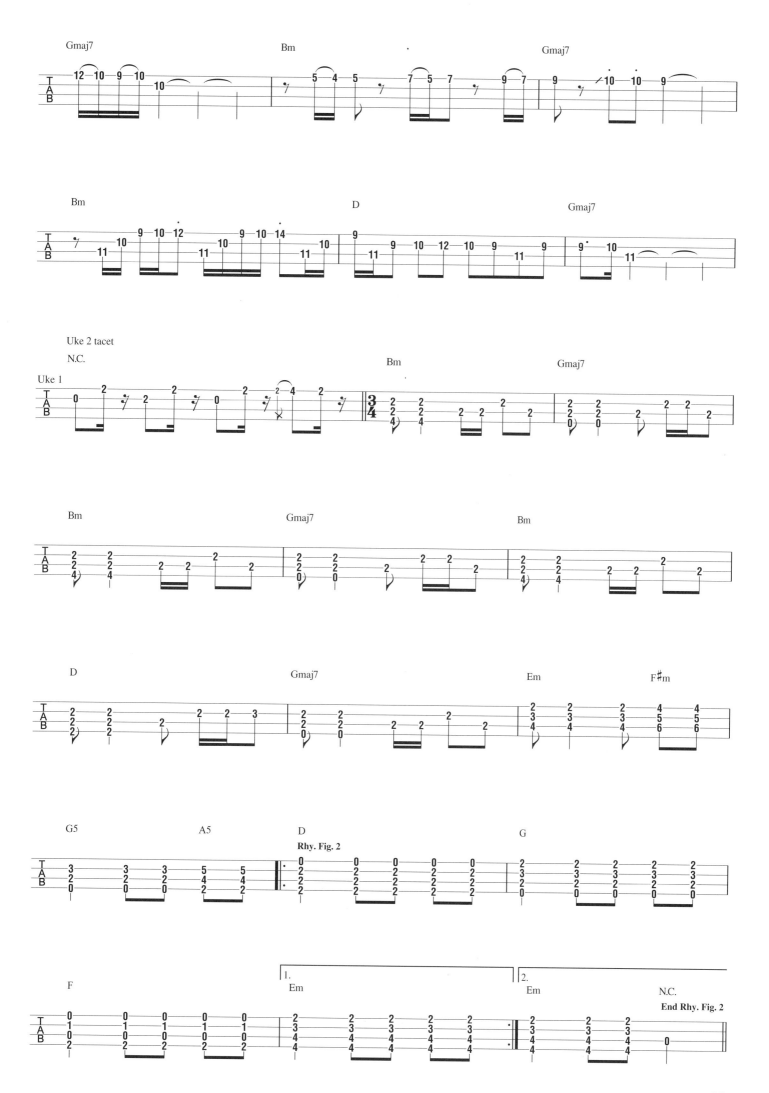

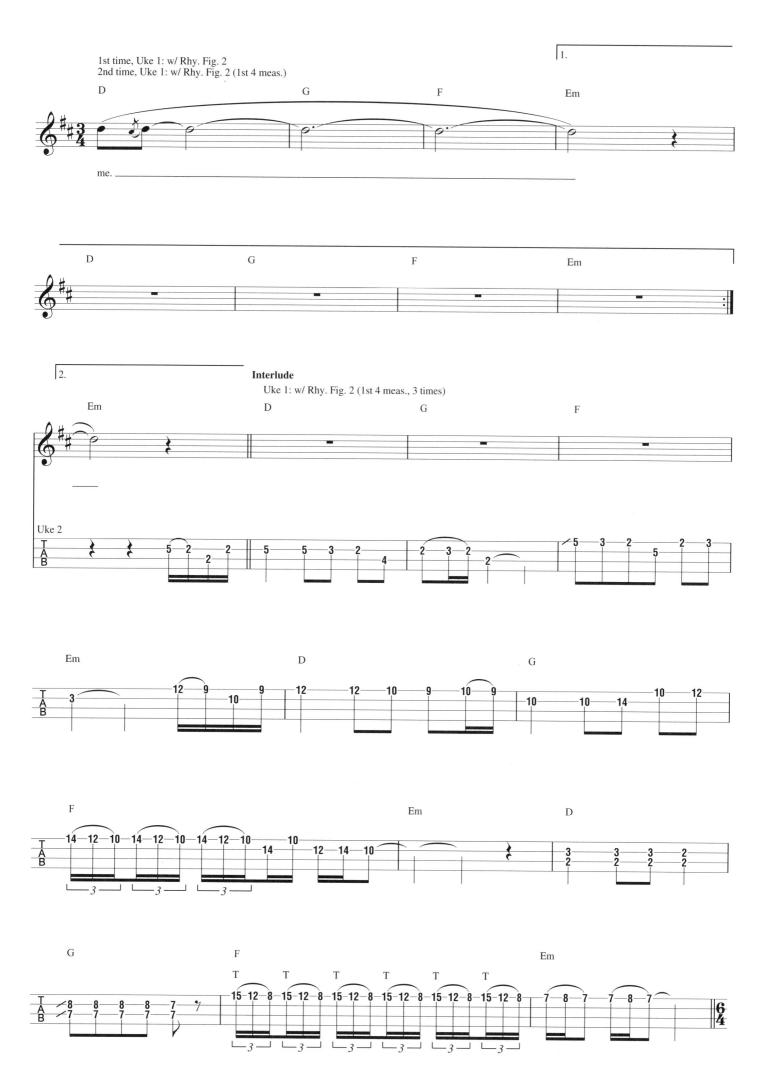

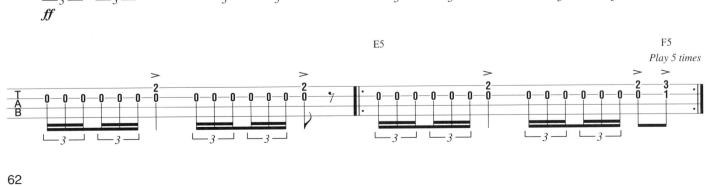

1. Dark - ness im - pris - on - ing me, all that I see, ab - so - lute hor - ror!
2. Land - mine has tak - en my sight, tak - en my speech, tak - en my hear - ing,

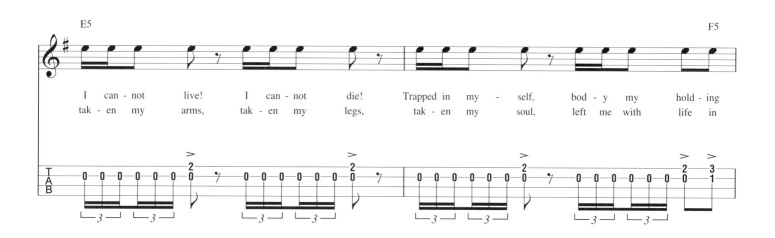

I can - not live! I can - not die! Trapped in my - self, bod - y my hold - ing
tak - en my arms, tak - en my legs, tak - en my soul, left me with life in

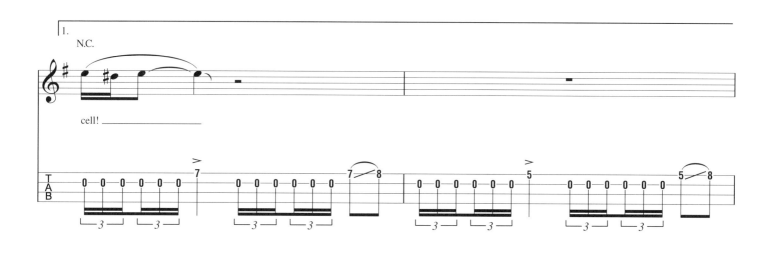

1.

N.C.

cell! _____

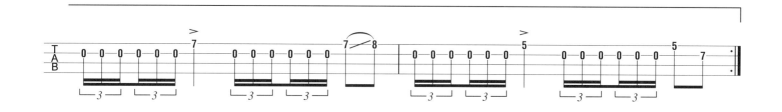

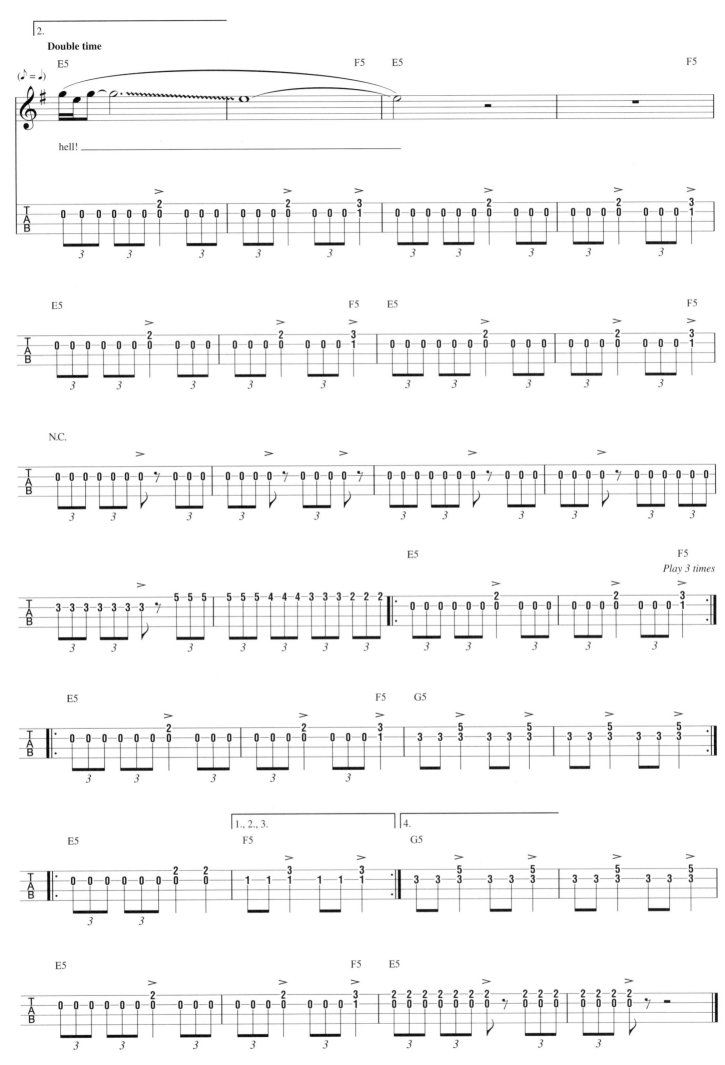

RIDE THE LIGHTNING

Words and Music by
James Hetfield, Lars Ulrich,
Cliff Burton and Dave Mustaine

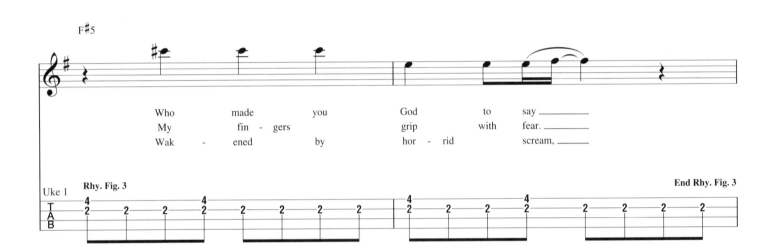

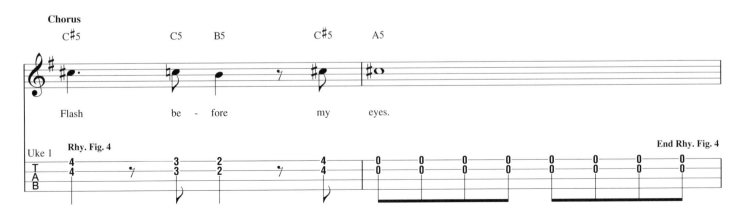

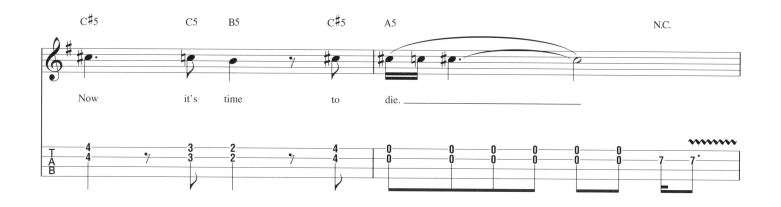

Now it's time to die. _____

Uke 1: w/ Rhy. Fig. 3

Uke 1: w/ Rhy. Fig. 4 (2 times)

Burn - ing in my brain.

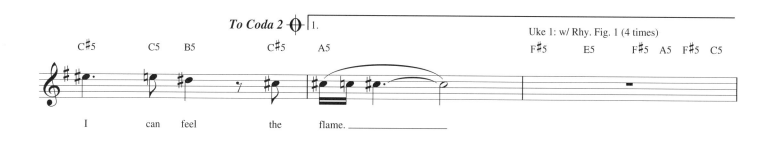

To Coda 2

I can feel the flame. _____

Uke 1: w/ Rhy. Fig. 1 (4 times)

flame. _____

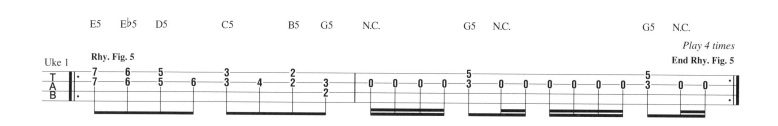

Uke 1

Rhy. Fig. 5

Play 4 times

End Rhy. Fig. 5

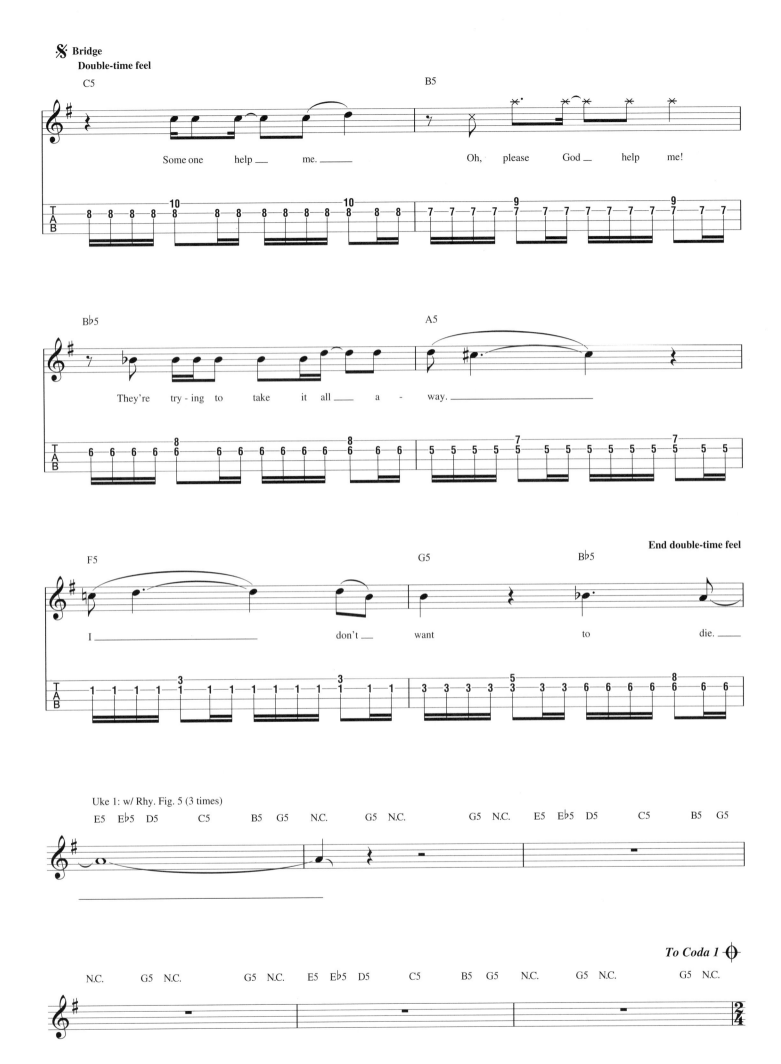

Half-time feel

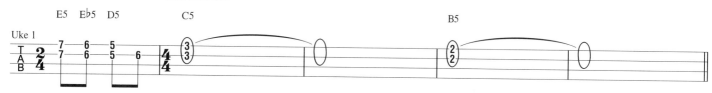

End half-time feel

Play 4 times

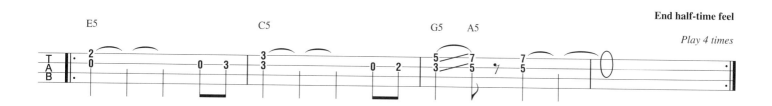

Play 4 times

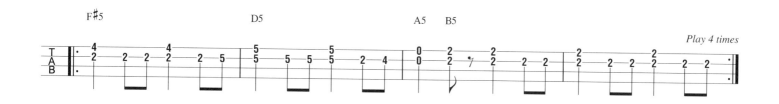

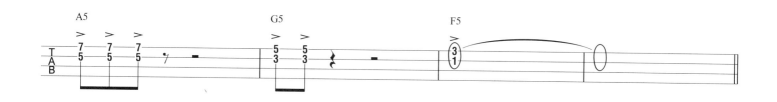

D.S. al Coda 1

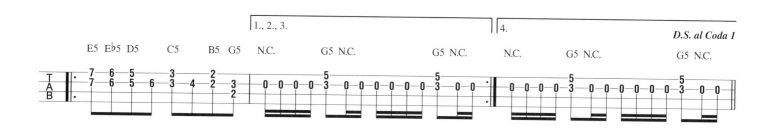

Coda 1

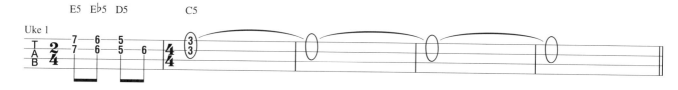

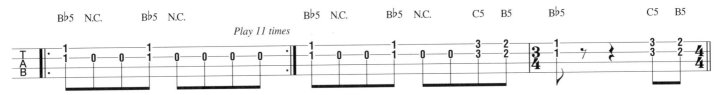

⊕ Coda 2

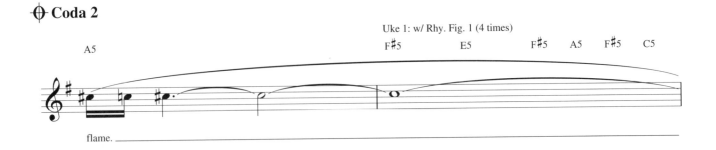

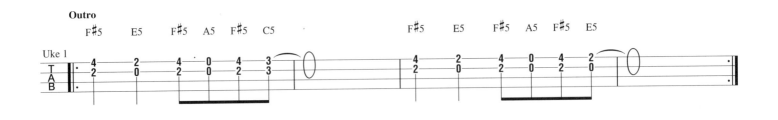

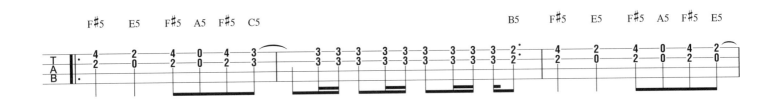

SAD BUT TRUE

Words and Music by
James Hetfield and Lars Ulrich

Tune down 1 step:
(low to high) F-Bb-D-G

Intro
Moderately slow Rock ♩ = 86

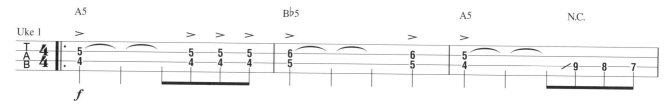

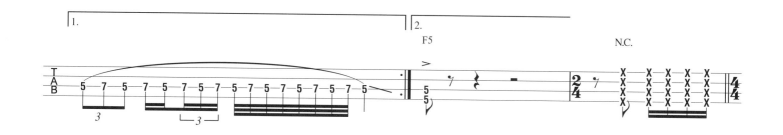

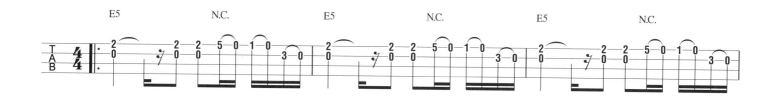

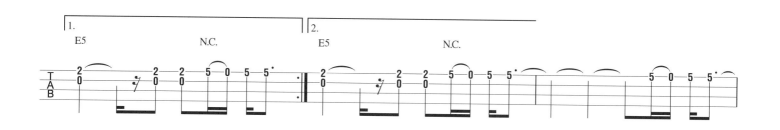

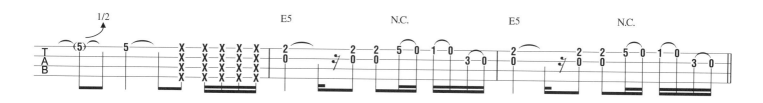

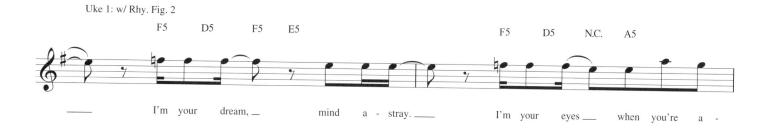

I'm your dream, ___ mind a - stray. ___ I'm your eyes ___ when you're a -

way. I'm your pain ___ while you re - pay. ___ You know it's sad but true. ___

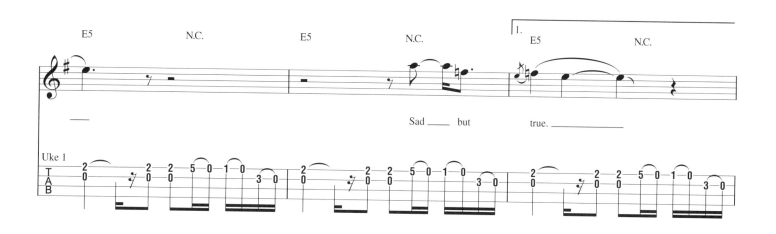

___ Sad ___ but true. ___

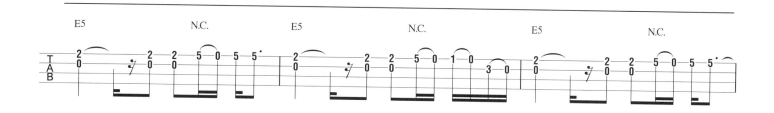

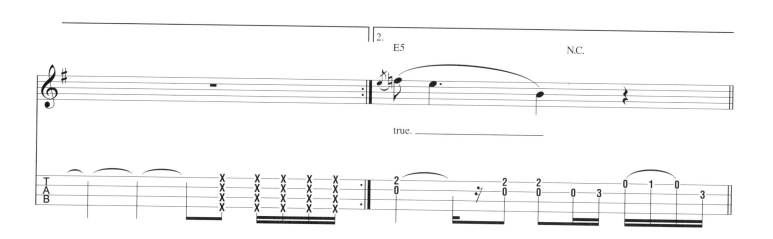

true. ___

Interlude

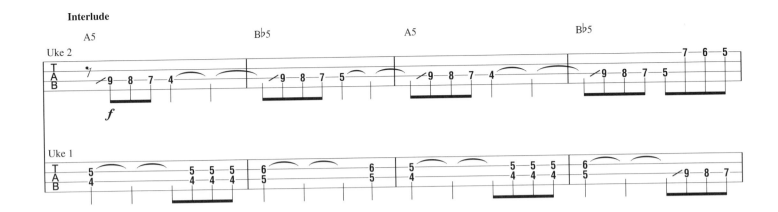

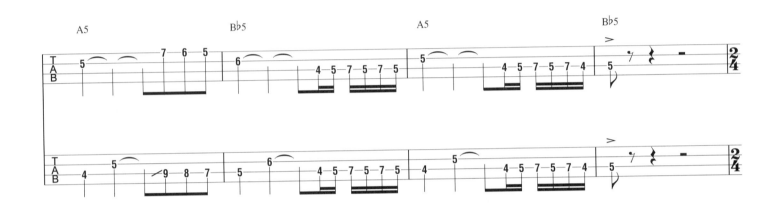

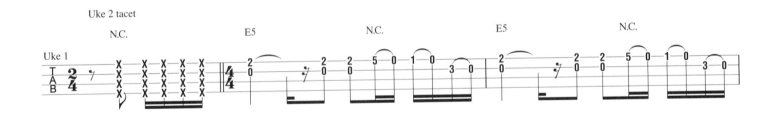

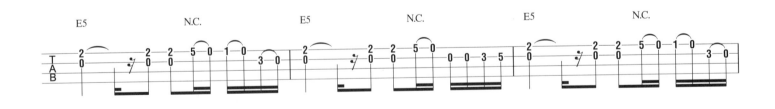

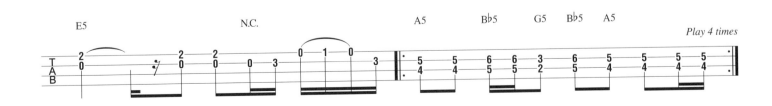

Bridge

Uke 1: w/ Rhy. Fig. 2 (2 times)

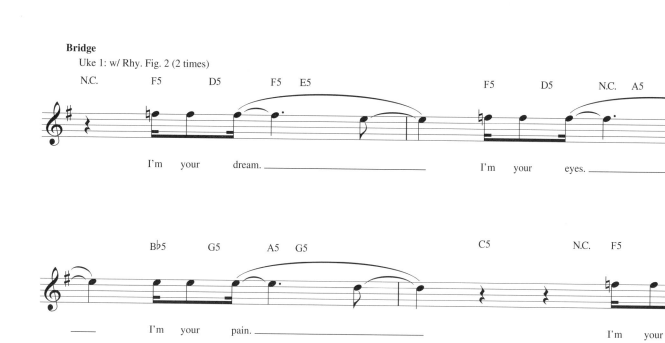

I'm your dream. _____ I'm your eyes. _____

_____ I'm your pain. _____ I'm your dream. __

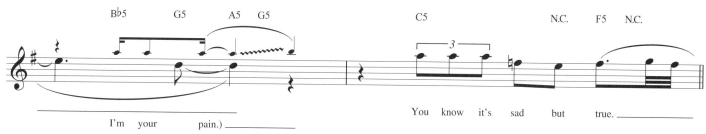

I'm your eyes. _____ I'm your pain. ___

(I'm your dream. _____ I'm your eyes. _____

I'm your pain.) _____ You know it's sad but true. _____

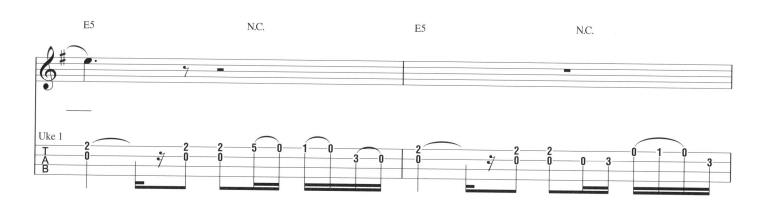

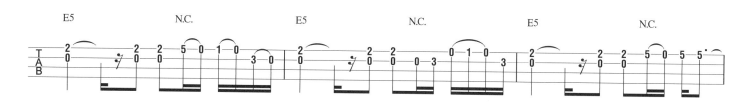

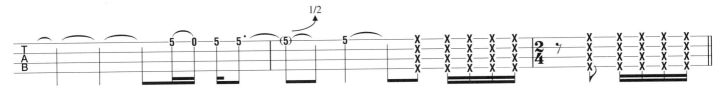

Coda

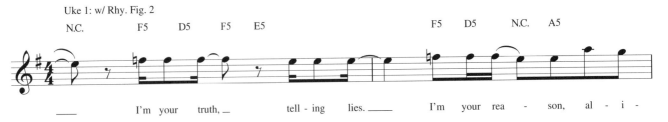

Uke 1: w/ Rhy. Fig. 2

N.C.　　　F5　D5　F5　E5　　　　　　　　　F5　D5　N.C.　A5

___ I'm your truth, ___ tell - ing lies. ___ I'm your rea - son, al - i -

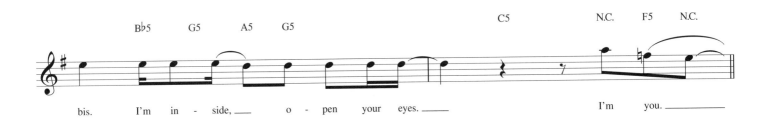

Bb5　　G5　　A5　　G5　　　　　　　　　　C5　　N.C.　F5　N.C.

bis. I'm in - side, ___ o - pen your eyes. ___ I'm you. _____

Outro

E5　　　　　N.C.　　　E5　　　　N.C.　　　E5　　　　　N.C.

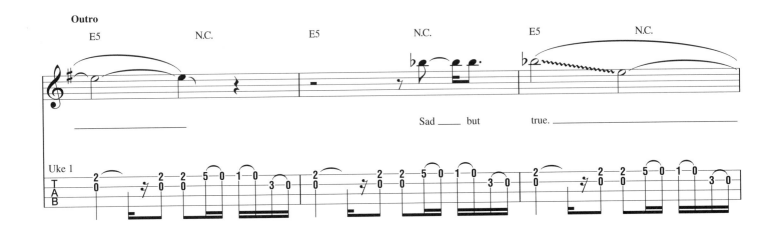

Sad ___ but　　true. ___

Uke 1

E5　　　　　　　N.C.　　　　　　　　　　　　E5

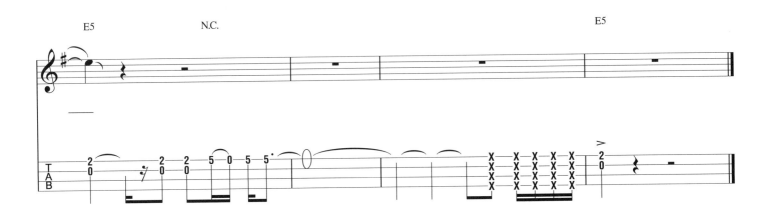

SEEK & DESTROY

Words and Music by
James Hetfield and Lars Ulrich

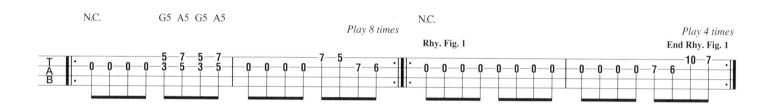

1. Scan-ning the scene ___ in the cit-y to-night. We're look-ing for you ___ to
   no es-cape ___ and that's for sure. This is the end; ___ we won't
   brains are on fire ___ with the feel-ing to kill, and it won't go a-way ___ un-til our

start up a fight. There's an e-vil feel-ing in our ___ brains, ___ but it's
take an-y-more. Say good-bye to the world you live in.
dreams are ful-filled. There is on-ly one thing on our ___ minds. ___ Don't try

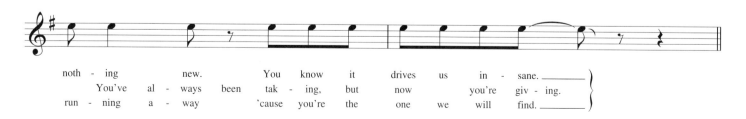

noth-ing new. You know it drives us in-sane. ___
You've al-ways been tak-ing, but now you're giv-ing.
run-ning a-way 'cause you're the one we will find. ___

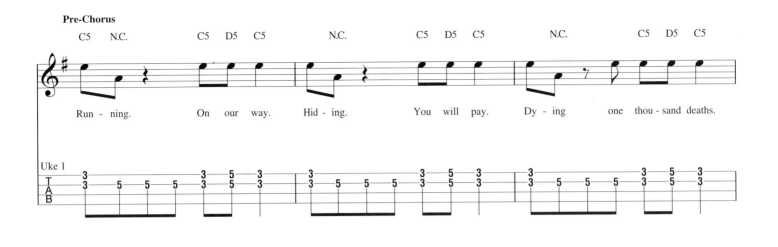

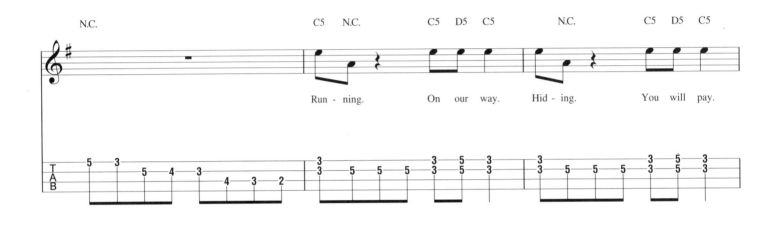

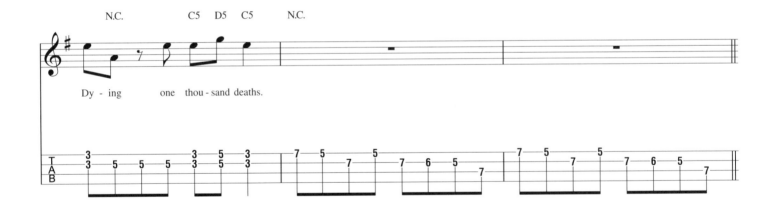

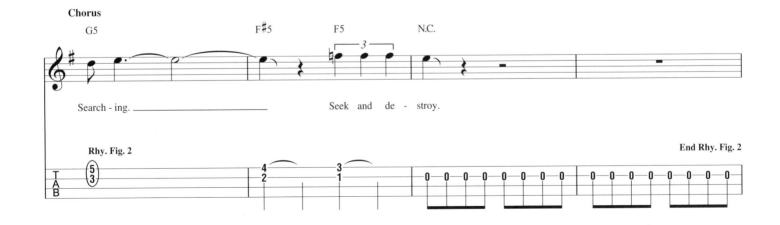

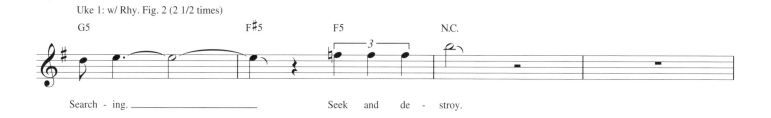

Uke 1: w/ Rhy. Fig. 2 (2 1/2 times)

Search - ing. Seek and de - stroy.

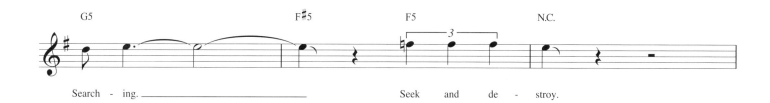

Search - ing. Seek and de - stroy.

To Coda 1

To Coda 2

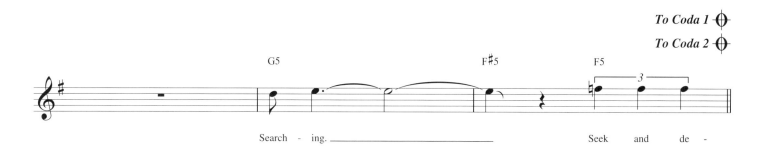

Search - ing. Seek and de -

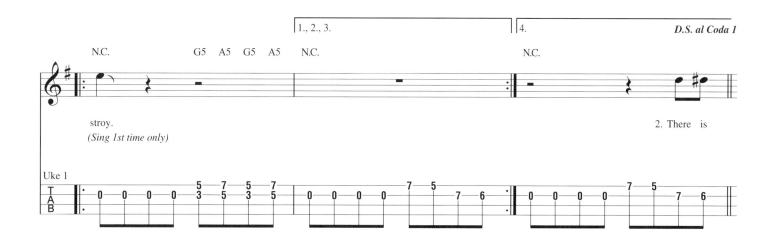

1., 2., 3.

4.

D.S. al Coda 1

stroy.
(Sing 1st time only)

2. There is

Coda 1

Faster ♩ = 208

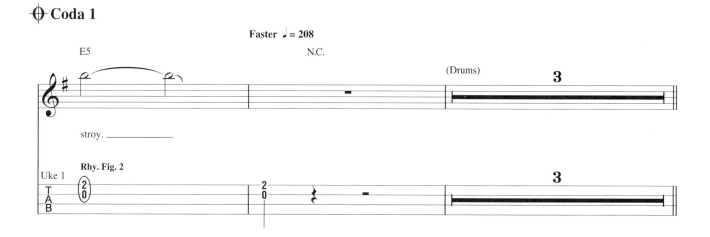

stroy.

Rhy. Fig. 2

Interlude

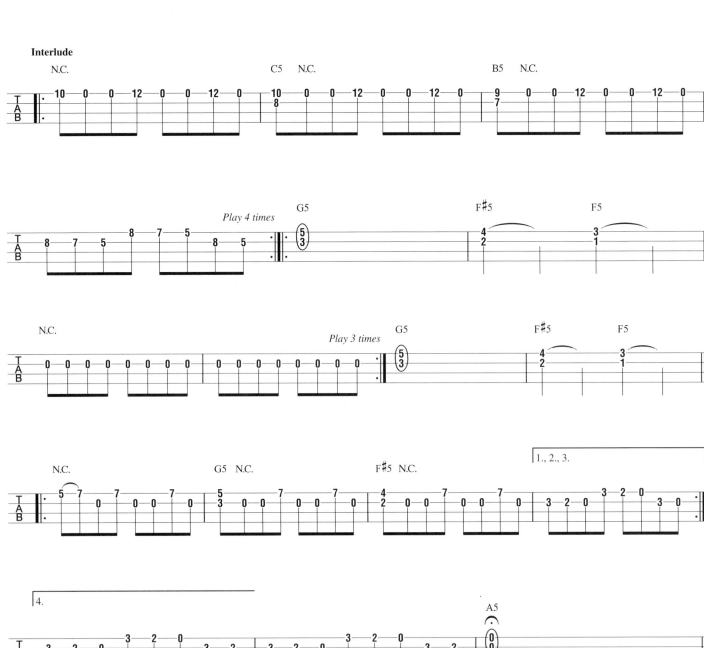

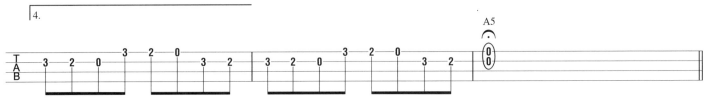

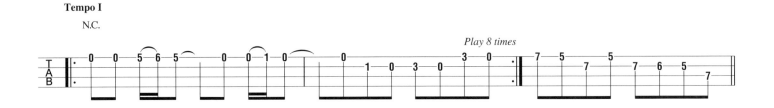

Tempo I

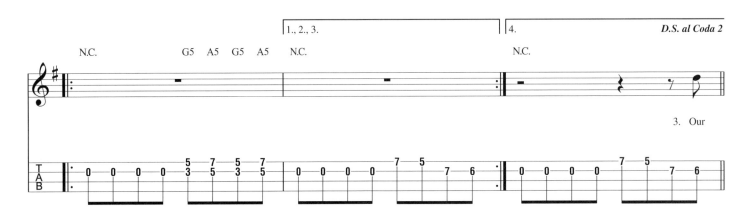

3. Our

80

Coda 2

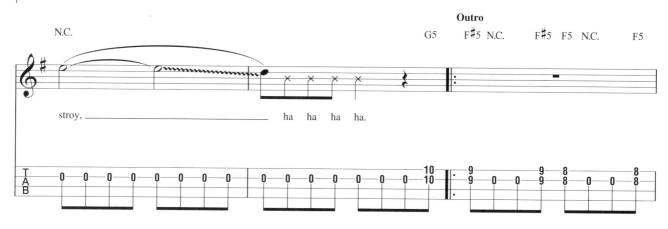

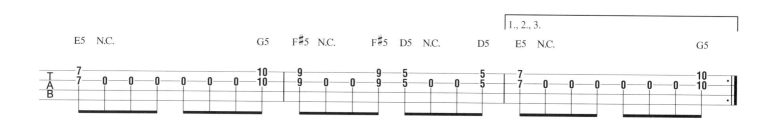

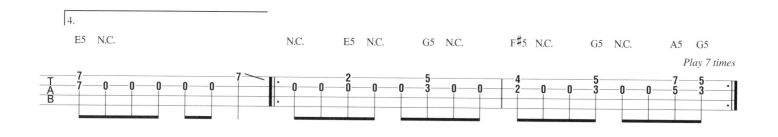

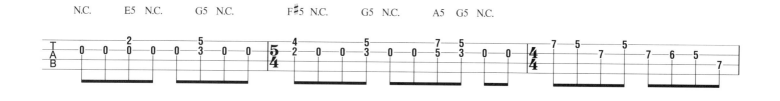

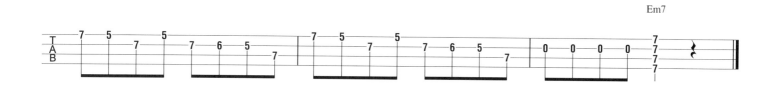

THE UNFORGIVEN

Words and Music by
James Hetfield, Lars Ulrich
and Kirk Hammett

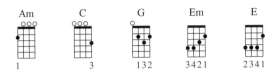

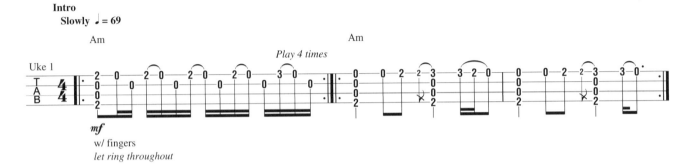

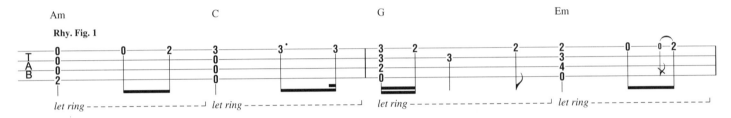

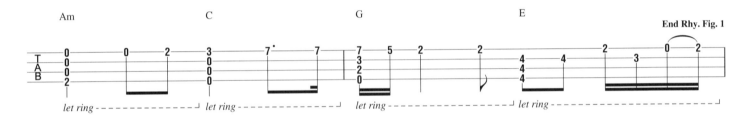

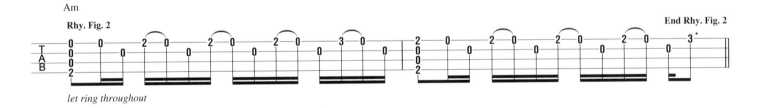

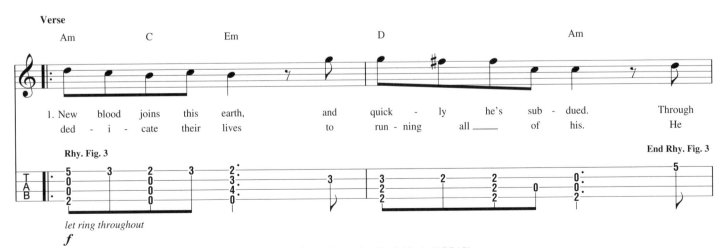

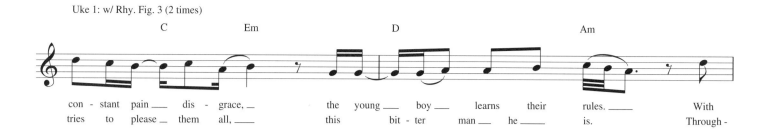

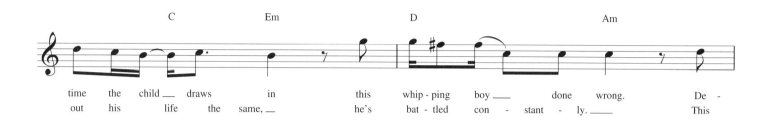

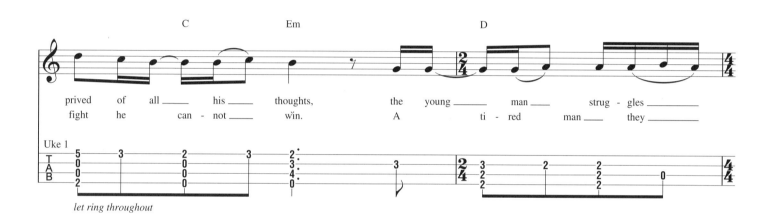

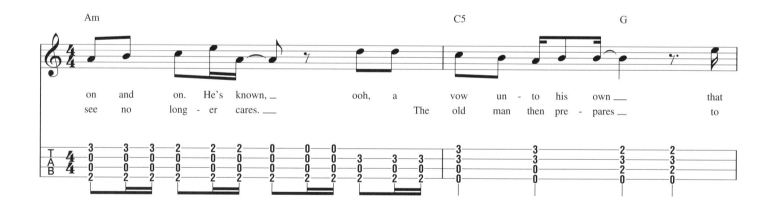

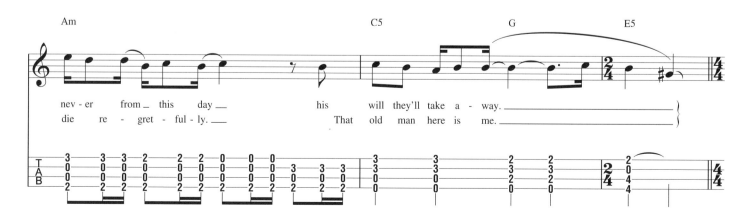

§ Chorus

Uke 1: w/ Rhy. Fig. 1 (2 times)

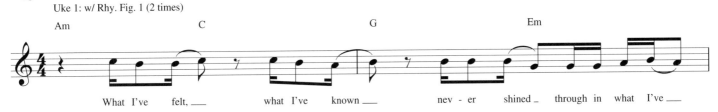

What I've felt, ___ what I've known ___ nev - er shined _ through in what I've ___

shown. Nev - er be. ___ Nev - er see. ___ Won't see what might _ have ___

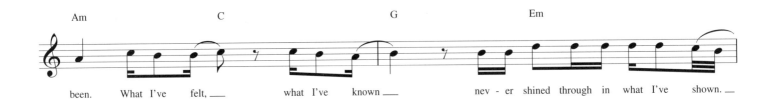

been. What I've felt, ___ what I've known ___ nev - er shined through in what I've shown. ___

To Coda ⊕

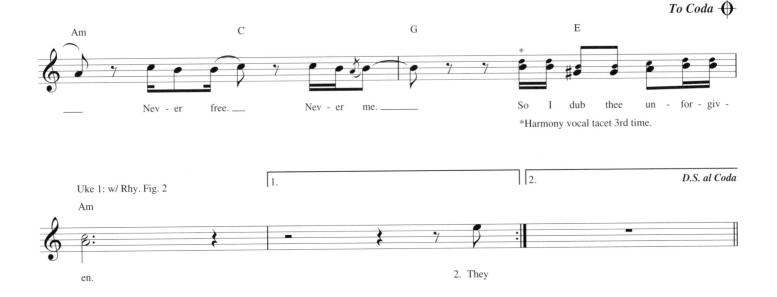

___ Nev - er free. ___ Nev - er me. ___ So I dub thee un - for - giv -

*Harmony vocal tacet 3rd time.

Uke 1: w/ Rhy. Fig. 2

1.   2.   *D.S. al Coda*

en.   2. They

⊕ **Coda**

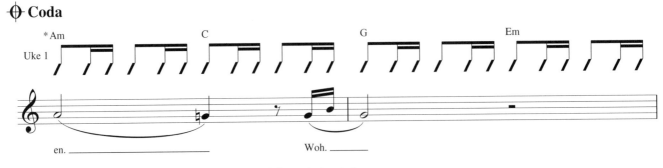

en. _____ Woh. ___

*See top of first page of song for chord diagrams pertaining to rhythm slashes.

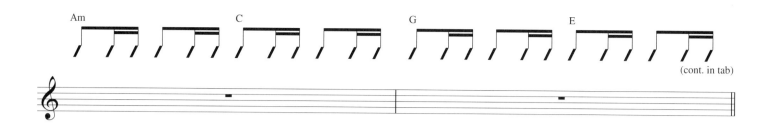

(cont. in tab)

Outro

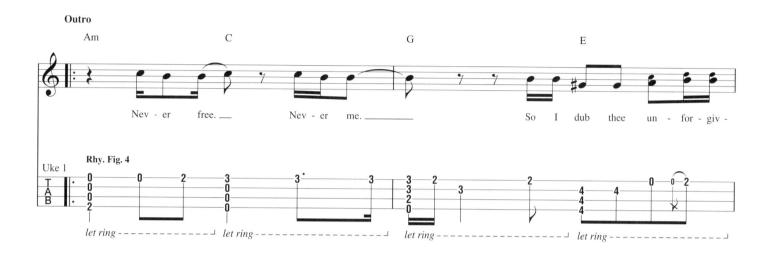

Nev - er free. ___ Nev - er me. ___ So I dub thee un - for - giv -

Uke 1

Rhy. Fig. 4

let ring ___ *let ring* ___ *let ring* ___ *let ring* ___

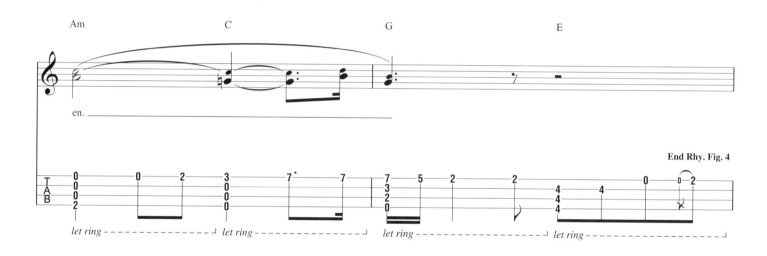

en. ___

End Rhy. Fig. 4

let ring ___ *let ring* ___ *let ring* ___ *let ring* ___

Uke 1: w/ Rhy. Fig. 4

You la - bled me. ___ I'll la - ble you. ___ So I dub thee un - for - giv -

Repeat and fade

en. ___

UNTIL IT SLEEPS

Words and Music by
James Hetfield and Lars Ulrich

Am

Tune down 1/2 step:
(low to high) G♭-C♭-E♭-A♭

Intro
Moderate Rock ♩ = 120

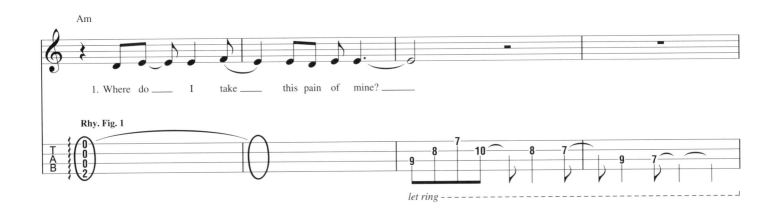

Chorus

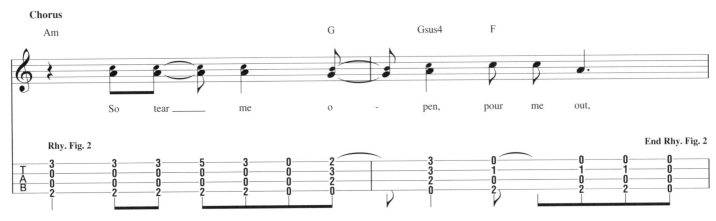

Uke 1: w/ Rhy. Fig. 2 (3 times)

there's things in - side that scream and shout. And the pain

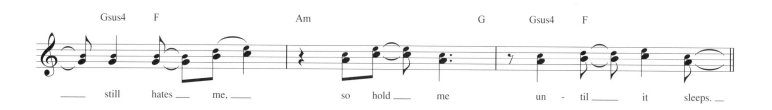

still hates me, so hold me un - til it sleeps.

Interlude

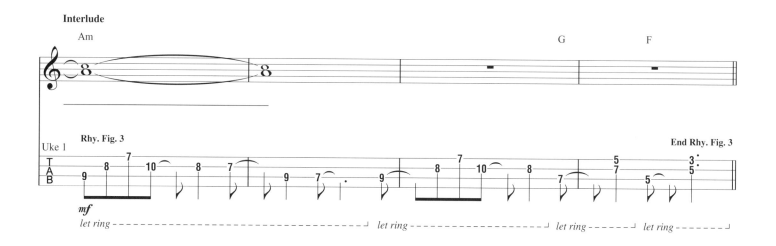

Uke 1

Rhy. Fig. 3

End Rhy. Fig. 3

let ring - - - - - - - - - - - - - - - - - - - *let ring* - - - - - - - - - - - - - *let ring* - - - - - - *let ring* - - - - - -

Verse

Uke 1: w/ Rhy. Fig. 1

2. Just like the curse, just like the stray.
3. So tell me why you've cho - sen me.

You feed it once and now it stays,
Don't want your grip, don't want your greed.

Chorus

Uke 1: w/ Rhy. Fig. 2 (4 times)

now it stays. So tear me o - pen, but be - ware,
Don't want it. I'll tear me o - pen, make you gone.

there's things _____ in - side _____ with - out _____ a care. _____
No more _____ can you _____ hurt an - y - one. _____

And the dirt _____
And the fear _____

_____ still stains _____ me, _____ so wash _____ me un - til _____ I'm clean. _____
_____ still shakes _____ me, _____ so hold _____ me un - til _____ it sleeps. _____

Bridge

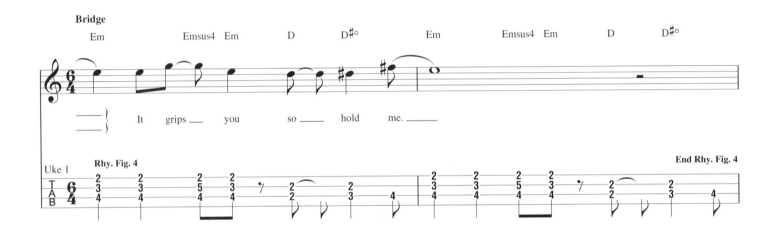

It grips _____ you so _____ hold me. _____

Uke 1

Rhy. Fig. 4

End Rhy. Fig. 4

Uke 1: w/ Rhy. Fig. 4 (3 times)

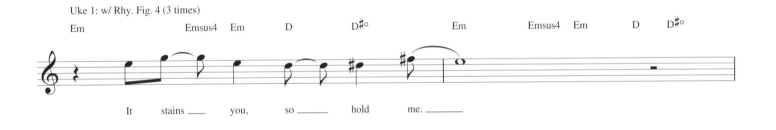

It stains _____ you, so _____ hold me. _____

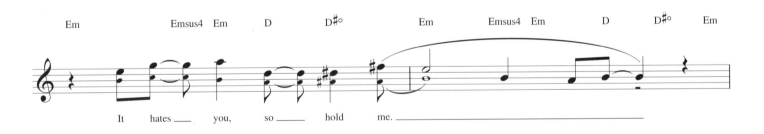

It hates _____ you, so _____ hold me.

1.

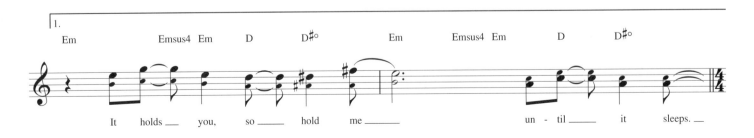

It holds _____ you, so _____ hold me _____ un - til _____ it sleeps. _____

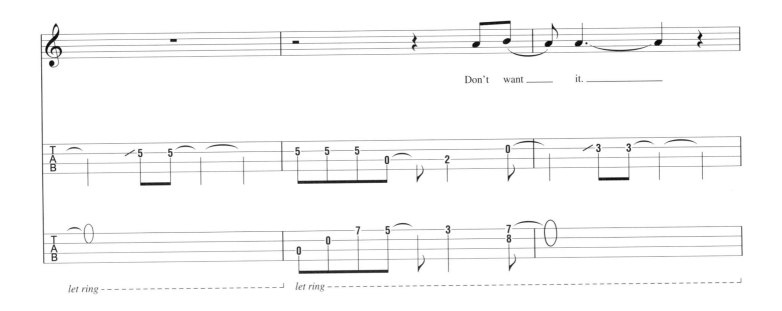

Don't want _____ it. _____

let ring - - - - - - - - - - - - - - - -   *let ring -*

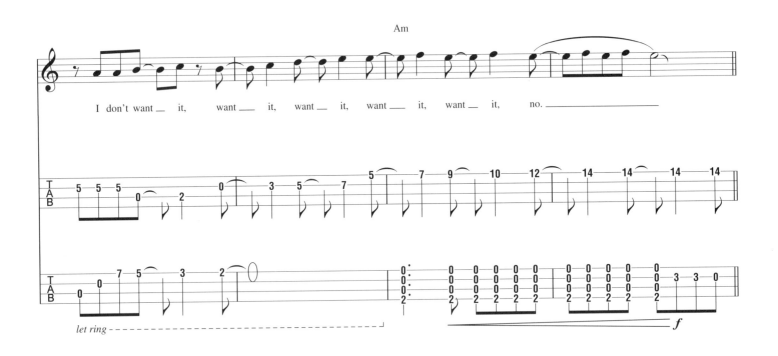

I don't want _ it, want _ it, want _ it, want _ it, want _ it, no. _____

let ring -

Chorus

Uke 1: w/ Rhy. Fig. 2 (8 times)
Uke 2 tacet

1. So tear _____ me o - pen, but be - ware,   there's things _____ in - side _____
2. I'll tear _____ me o - pen, make you gone.   No long - er will you _____

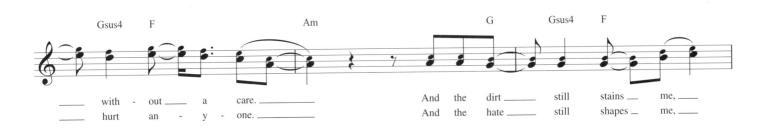

_____ with - out _____ a care. _____   And the dirt _____ still stains _____ me, _____
_____ hurt an - y - one. _____   And the hate _____ still shapes _ me, _____

90

so wash ___ me   till I'm clean. ___   un - til ___ it   sleeps, ___
so hold ___ me

Outro

Un - til ___ it   sleeps, ___   Un - til ___ it   sleeps. ___

un - til ___ it   sleeps. ___   un - til ___ it   sleeps. ___

WELCOME HOME
(SANITARIUM)

Words and Music by
James Hetfield, Lars Ulrich
and Kirk Hammett

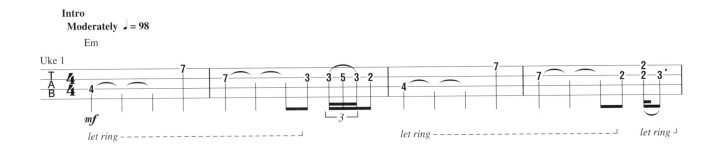

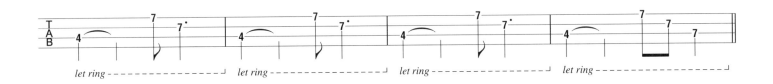

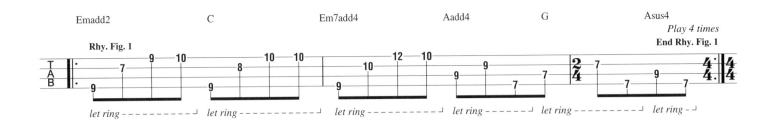

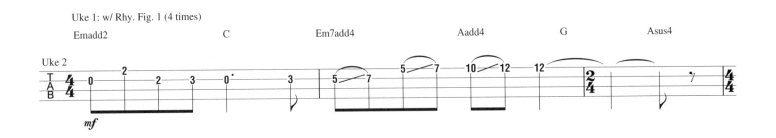

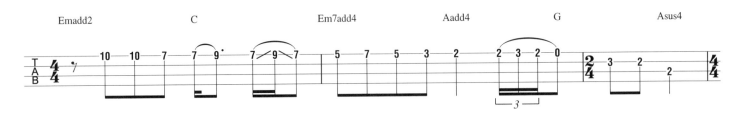

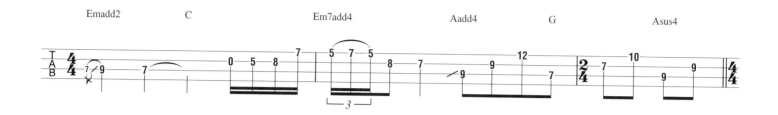

Verse

Uke 1: w/ Rhy. Fig. 1 (4 times)

Uke 2 tacet

1. Wel - come to where time stands still. No one leaves and no ____ one will. ____
2. Build my fear of what's ___ out there; ___ can - not breathe the o - pen air. ____

Moon is full, ___ nev - er seems to change. ___ Just la - beled men - tal - ly ____ de - ranged. ____
Whis - per things in - to ____ my brain, ___ as - sur - ing me that I'm ___ in - sane. ____ They

*Sing harmony voc. 2nd time only.

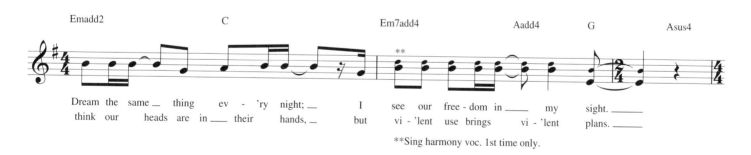

Dream the same ___ thing ev - 'ry night; ___ I see our free - dom in ____ my sight. ____
think our heads are in ___ their hands, ___ but vi - 'lent use brings vi - 'lent plans. ____

**Sing harmony voc. 1st time only.

No locked doors, no win - dows barred, ___ no things to make ___ my brain seem scarred. ____
Keep him tied; it makes ___ him well. ___ He's get - ting bet - ter; can't you tell? ____

Pre-Chorus

Sleep, my friend, and you will see ___ that dream is my re - al - i - ty. ___ They
No more can they keep us in. ___ Lis - ten, damn it, we will win. ___ They

P.M. ------------------------------ P.M. ------ P.M.

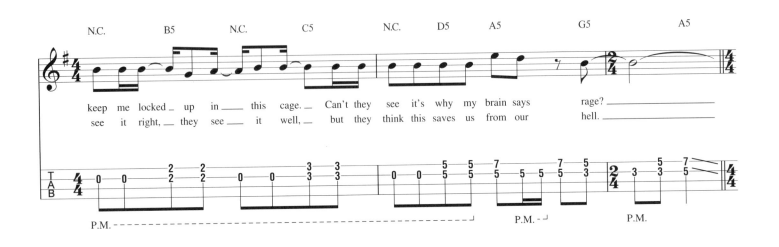

keep me locked ___ up in ___ this cage. ___ Can't they see it's why my brain says rage? ___
see it right, ___ they see ___ it well, ___ but they think this saves us from our hell. ___

P.M. -- P.M. -- P.M.

Chorus

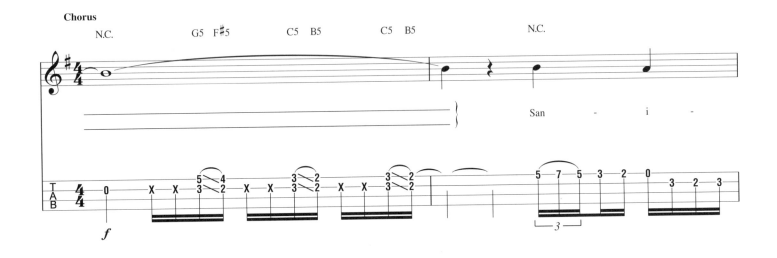

San - i -

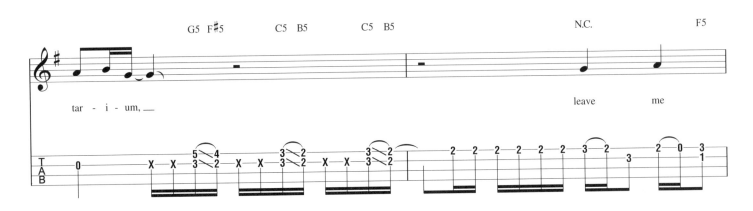

tar - i - um, ___ leave me

94

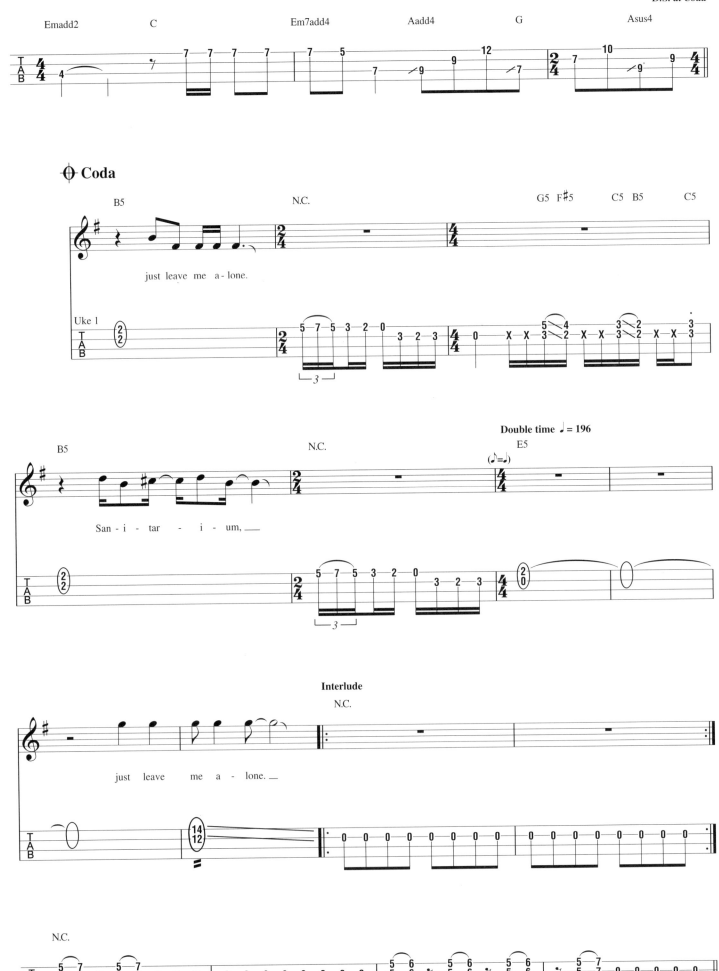

Play 3 times

Bridge
Tempo I ♩ = 98

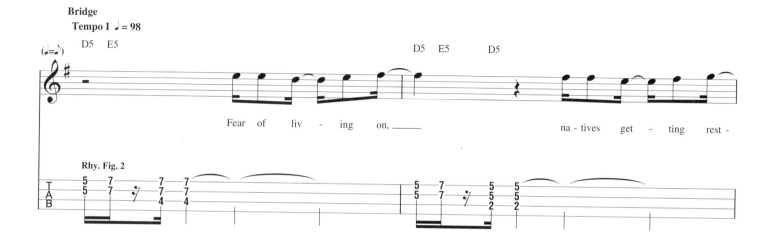

Fear of liv - ing on, _____ na - tives get - ting rest -

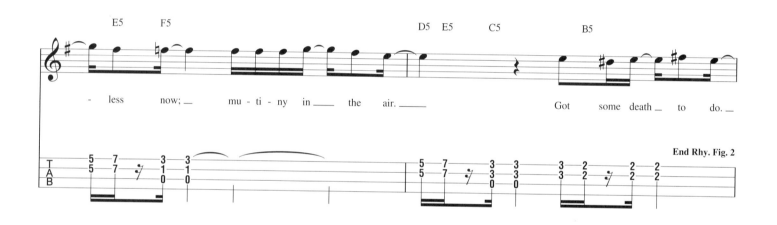

- less now; ___ mu - ti - ny in ___ the air. ___ Got some death ___ to do. ___

Uke 1: w/ Rhy. Fig. 2

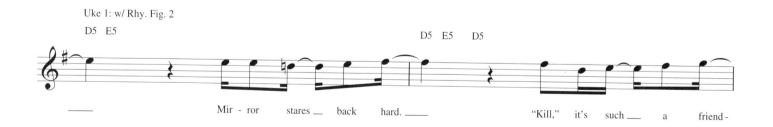

___ Mir - ror stares ___ back hard. _____ "Kill," it's such ___ a friend -

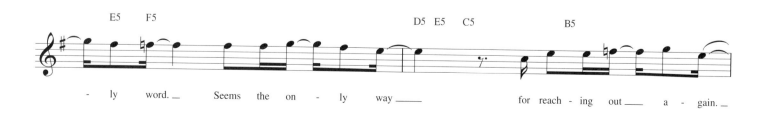

- ly word. ___ Seems the on - ly way _____ for reach - ing out ___ a - gain. ___

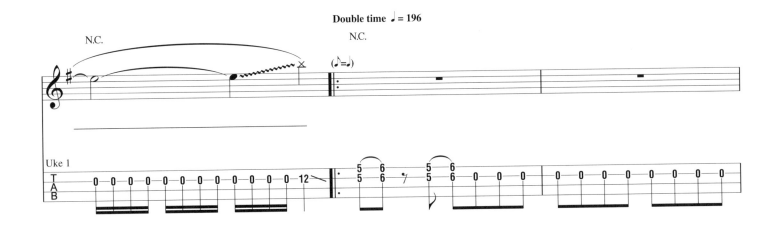

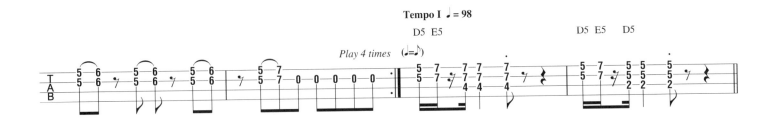

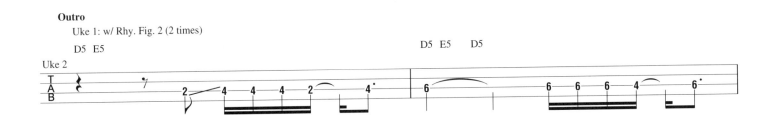

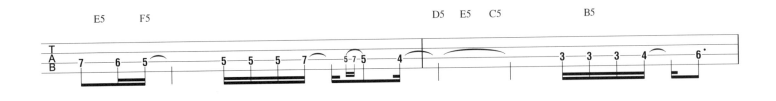

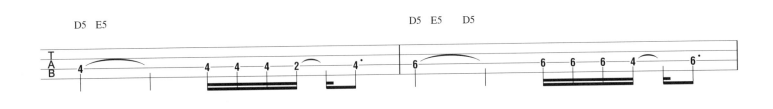

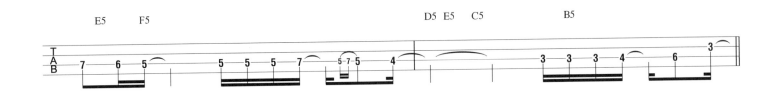

Uke 1: w/ Rhy. Fig. 2 (2 times)

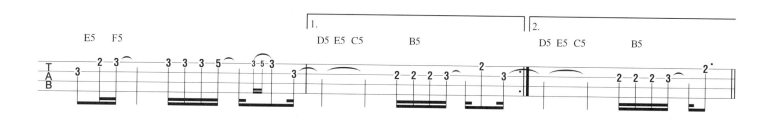

Uke 2 tacet

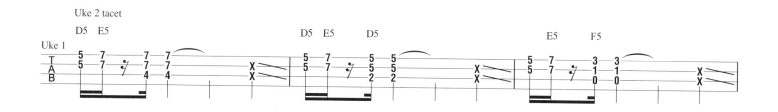

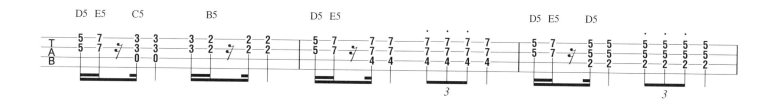

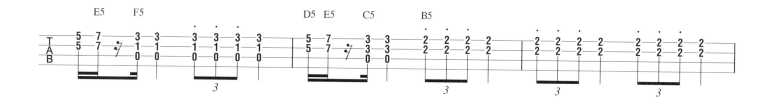

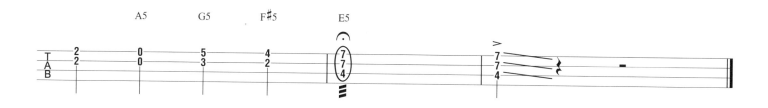

WHEREVER I MAY ROAM

Words and Music by
James Hetfield and Lars Ulrich

To the game you stay a slave. _____
Off the beat - en path I reign. _____

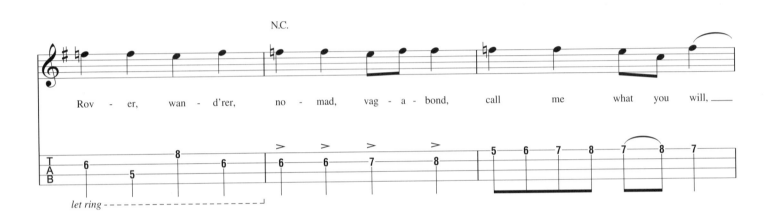

Rov - er, wan - d'rer, no - mad, vag - a - bond, call me what you will, _____

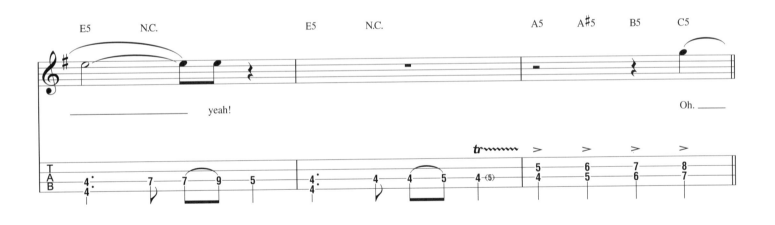

yeah! Oh. _____

Pre-Chorus

But I'll take my time an - y - where, free to

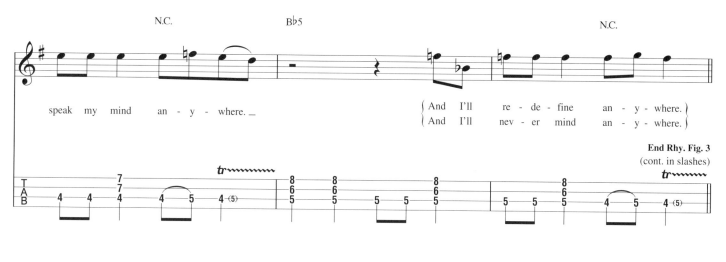

speak my mind an-y-where. ___

And I'll re-de-fine an-y-where.
And I'll nev-er mind an-y-where.

End Rhy. Fig. 3
(cont. in slashes)

Chorus

Half-time feel

To Coda ⊕
End half-time feel

End Rhy. Fig. 4
(cont. in tab)

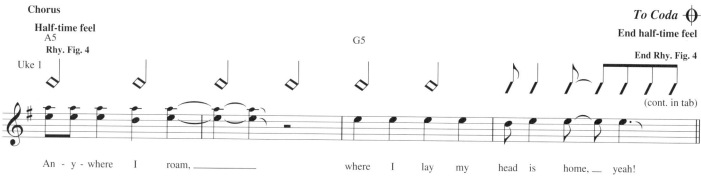

An-y-where I roam, ___ where I lay my head is home, ___ yeah!

Half-time feel

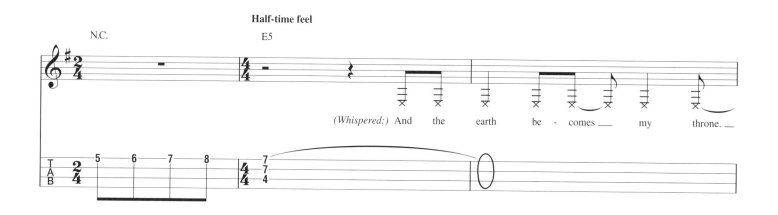

(Whispered:) And the earth be-comes ___ my throne. ___

D.S. al Coda

2. And the earth be-comes ___ my throne. ___

let ring - - - - - - - - - -

Coda

Interlude

Pre-Chorus

Uke 1: w/ Rhy. Fig. 3

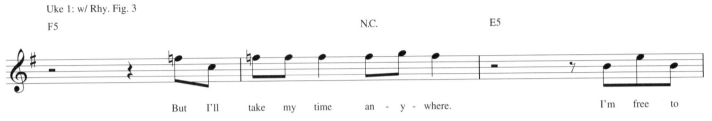

But I'll take my time an - y - where.   I'm free to

speak my mind. ___   And I'll take my find an - y - where.

Chorus

Half-time feel

Uke 1: w/ Rhy. Fig. 4

End half-time feel

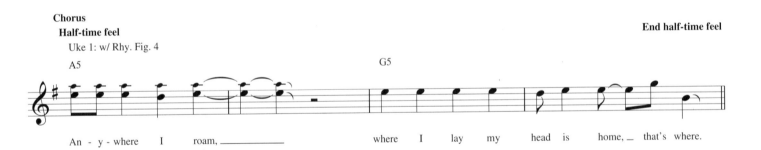

An - y - where I roam, ___   where I lay my head is home, ___ that's where.

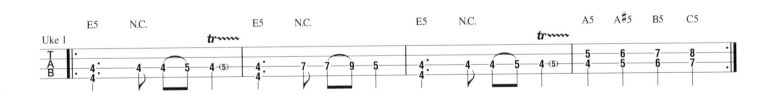

Pre-Chorus

Uke 1: w/ Rhy. Fig. 3

But I'll take my time an - y - where.   I'm free to

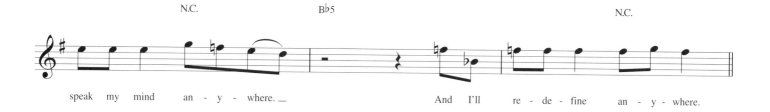

speak my mind an - y - where. ___ And I'll re - de - fine an - y - where.

Chorus
Half-time feel

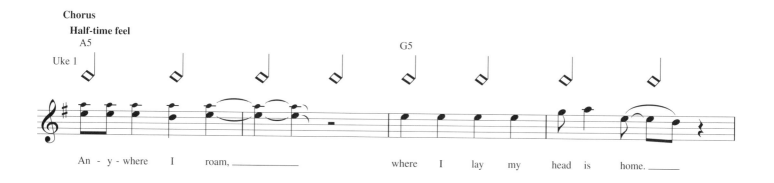

An - y - where I roam, _____ where I lay my head is home. _____

Carved up - on ___ my stone, ___ my bod - y ___ lie, ___ but still I ___ roam, _ yeah, _ yeah. _

Outro
Uke 1: w/ Rhy. Fig. 1

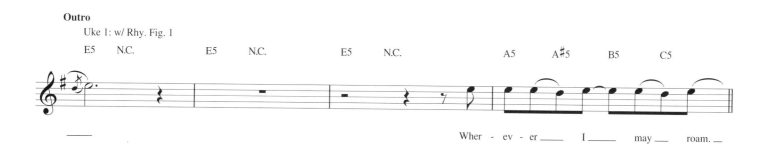

___ Wher - ev - er ___ I ___ may ___ roam. _

Uke 1: w/ Rhy. Fig. 2

Repeat and fade

___ Wher - ev - er ___ I ___ may roam. _

STRUM & SING

WITH

cherry lane
music company

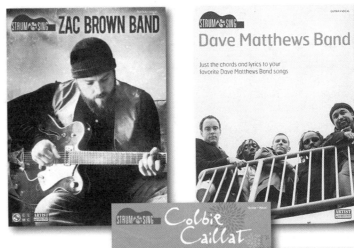

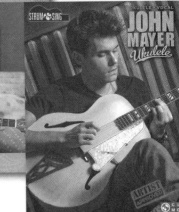

GUITAR

SARA BAREILLES
00102354...$12.99

ZAC BROWN BAND
02501620...$12.99

COLBIE CAILLAT
02501725...$14.99

CAMPFIRE FOLK SONGS
02500686...$10.99

CHRISTMAS CAROLS
02500631...$6.95

COUNTRY
02500755...$9.95

JOHN DENVER COLLECTION
02500632...$9.95

50 CHILDREN'S SONGS
02500825...$7.95

THE 5 CHORD SONGBOOK
02501718...$9.99

FOLK SONGS
02501482...$9.99

FOLK/ROCK FAVORITES
02501669...$9.99

40 POP/ROCK HITS
02500633...$9.95

THE 4 CHORD SONGBOOK
02501533...$10.99

HITS OF THE '60S
02501138...$10.95

HITS OF THE '70S
02500871...$9.99

HYMNS
02501125...$8.99

JACK JOHNSON
02500858...$14.99

DAVE MATTHEWS BAND
02501078...$10.95

JOHN MAYER
02501636...$10.99

INGRID MICHAELSON
02501634...$10.99

THE MOST REQUESTED SONGS
02501748...$10.99

JASON MRAZ
02501452...$14.99

ROCK BALLADS
02500872...$9.95

THE 6 CHORD SONGBOOK
02502277...$10.99

UKULELE

COLBIE CAILLAT
02501731...$10.99

JOHN DENVER
02501694...$10.99

JACK JOHNSON
02501752...$10.99

JOHN MAYER
02501706...$10.99

INGRID MICHAELSON
02501741...$10.99

THE MOST REQUESTED SONGS
02501453...$10.99

JASON MRAZ
02501753...$14.99

SING-ALONG SONGS
02501710...$10.99

See your local music dealer or contact:

cherry lane
music company

EXCLUSIVELY DISTRIBUTED BY

HAL•LEONARD
CORPORATION

7777 W. BLUEMOUND RD. P.O. BOX 13819 MILWAUKEE, WI 53213

Prices, content, and availability subject to change
without notice.

0512

METALLICA

Visit Cherry Lane Online at
www.cherrylane.com

MATCHING FOLIOS

...AND JUSTICE FOR ALL
02506965	Play-It-Like-It-Is Guitar	$22.99
02506982	Play-It-Like-It-Is Bass	$19.95
02506856	Easy Guitar	$12.95
02503504	Drums	$18.95

DEATH MAGNETIC
02501267	Play-It-Like-It-Is Guitar	$24.95
02501312	Play-It-Like-It-Is Bass	$22.95
02501316	Easy Guitar	$15.95
02501315	Drums	$19.99

GARAGE INC.
02500070	Play-It-Like-It-Is Guitar	$24.95
02500075	Play-It-Like-It-Is Bass	$24.95
02500076	Easy Guitar	$14.95
02500077	Drums	$18.95

KILL 'EM ALL
02507018	Play-It-Like-It-Is Guitar	$19.99
02507039	Play-It-Like-It-Is Bass	$19.95

LIVE: BINGE AND PURGE
02501232	Play-It-Like-It-Is Guitar	$19.95

LOAD
02501275	Play-It-Like-It-Is-Guitar	$24.95

MASTER OF PUPPETS
02507920	Play-It-Like-It-Is Guitar	$19.95
02506961	Play-It-Like-It-Is Bass	$19.95
02506859	Easy Guitar	$12.95
02503502	Drums	$18.95

METALLICA
02501195	Play-It-Like-It-Is Guitar	$22.95
02505911	Play-It-Like-It-Is Bass	$19.99
02506869	Easy Guitar	$14.95
02503509	Drums	$18.95

RE-LOAD
02501297	Play-It-Like-It-Is Guitar	$24.95
02503517	Drums	$18.95

RIDE THE LIGHTNING
02507019	Play-It-Like-It-Is Guitar	$19.95
02507040	Play-It-Like-It-Is Bass	$17.95
02506861	Easy Guitar	$12.95
02503507	Drums	$17.95

ST. ANGER
02500638	Play-It-Like-It-Is Guitar	$24.95
02500639	Play-It-Like-It-Is Bass	$19.95

S&M HIGHLIGHTS
02500279	Play-It-Like-It-Is Guitar	$24.95
02500288	Play-It-Like-It-Is Bass	$19.95

PLAYERS

THE ART OF KIRK HAMMETT
02506325	Guitar Transcriptions	$17.95

THE ART OF JAMES HETFIELD
02500016	Guitar Transcriptions	$17.95

METALLICA'S LARS ULRICH
Book/CD Pack
02506306	Drum	$17.95

COLLECTIONS

BEST OF METALLICA
02500424	Transcribed Full Scores	$24.95

BEST OF METALLICA
02502204	P/V/G	$17.95

METALLICA: CLASSIC SONGS
NOTE-FOR-NOTE TRANSCRIPTIONS WITH DVD
Book/DVD Packs
02501626	Guitar	$19.99
02501627	Bass	$19.99
02501625	Drum	$19.99

5 OF THE BEST
02506210	Play-It-Like-It-Is Guitar – Vol. 1	$12.95
02506235	Play-It-Like-It-Is Guitar – Vol. 2	$12.95

LEGENDARY LICKS
AN INSIDE LOOK AT THE STYLES OF METALLICA
Book/CD Packs
02500181	Guitar 1983-1988	$22.95
02500182	Guitar 1988-1996	$22.95
02500180	Bass Legendary Licks	$19.95
02500172	Drum Legendary Licks	$19.95

LEGENDARY LICKS DVDS
A STEP-BY-STEP BREAKDOWN OF
METALLICA'S STYLES AND TECHNIQUES
02500479	Guitar 1983-1988	$16.99
02500480	Guitar 1988-1997	$24.99
02500481	Bass 1983-1988	$16.99
02500484	Bass 1988-1997	$16.99
02500482	Drums 1983-1988	$16.99
02500485	Drums 1988-1997	$16.99

RIFF BY RIFF
02506313	Guitar Volume 1	$19.95
02500654	Guitar Volume 2	$19.95
02506328	Bass	$19.95

INSTRUCTION

METALLICA – EASY GUITAR WITH LESSONS
02506877	Volume 1	$14.95
02500419	Volume 2	$14.95

LEARN TO PLAY WITH METALLICA
Book/CD Packs
02500138	Guitar Volume 1	$15.95
02500885	Guitar Volume 2	$15.95
02500189	Bass Volume 1	$15.95
02500886	Bass Volume 2	$15.95
02500190	Drums	$14.95

UNDER THE MICROSCOPE
02500655	Guitar Instruction	$19.95

REFERENCE

METALLICA – THE COMPLETE LYRICS – SECOND EDITIONS
02501234	Lyrics	$9.99